BOOK TWO IN A SERIES

ANCIENT PATHS *for* MODERN WOMEN

Walking as Wives

JUDY GERR.

ISBN 0-9718306-3-0

Published by LifeSong Publishers
P.O. Box 183, Somis, CA 93066-0183
805-655-5644
www.lifesongpublishers.com

Unless otherwise noted, all Bible quotations used in this study are taken from the New American Standard Bible.

Webster's New World College Dictionary, Third Edition, Simon & Schuster, Inc., 1997.

Illustrations by Wendy Kappen
Cover design by Jeff Sharpton and Jon Walusiak at Design Point
Cover photo by Comstock.com
Printed in the United States of America

First Edition
Library of Congress Control Number: 2003111865
p.112 cm. 25.4

TABLE OF CONTENTS

Endorsements

"Being born female in today's Western world frequently offers a false sense of confidence. Armed with education and unprecedented privilege, women are writing their own scripts about family and personal fulfillment, but later encounter confusion and bleak emptiness. Having been taught to disregard the wisdom of their Creator, they bypass the solutions they seek.

Judy Gerry has dug deeply into the sacred records of the Bible to surface divine guidance for women in every generation. Here is a timely, reassuring and professionally crafted study resource which belongs in every church library and on the study agenda for thinking women."

Howard G. Hendricks
Distinguished Professor and Chairman, Center for Christian Leadership
Dallas Theological Seminary

"Judy Gerry has a long-time track record of walking with the Lord as a woman and as a wife and mother. For many years, she has had an effective ministry of training women in the Word and ways of God. Now her years of study and experience are combined in this practical and interactive course designed to help women understand God's purpose and plan for their lives.

Judy does not claim to offer new or original ideas. Rather, she leads women to discover and apply the tried, true, and enduring way laid out for us in the Scripture–the pathway that leads to blessing and joy.

In a day when so many Christian women are floundering and confused, the wisdom found in this program is timely and desperately needed. I pray this course will be widely received and will be used to bring about a true revolution in the hearts and homes of women who profess to know Christ."

Nancy Leigh DeMoss
Author; Host of Revive Our Hearts Radio

"I love *Ancient Paths for Modern Women* because it takes women to the Bible! His Word changes lives! I have observed tearful testimonies of women coming to Christ, marriages healed, children raised according to God's plan, repentance revived, and church problems solved. Today's women are so thirsty to hear God's Word. After teaching *Ancient Paths* this summer to forty women, I again stand in awe as I have watched God work through this study."

Linda Campbell
Bible Study Leader
Actively Serving in Women's Ministries in Ventura County

Preface

Millennia ago God set out ancient paths for us to walk, which would lead to abundant life, and into perfect fellowship with Himself. The Lord promised us that when we see and walk in that "good way," we will find rest for our souls.

"Thus says the LORD,
'Stand by the ways and see and ask for the ancient paths,
Where the good way is, and walk in it;
And you will find rest for your souls.'"
Jeremiah 6:16

Contemporary women have veered sharply from the "good way" that God has intended for us to live. While longing for elusive rest for their souls, women have rejected God's pathways as being too simplistic and archaic. Sensing that something is wrong, we are unable to grasp how grossly off track we are.

Many Christian women have "stumbled from the ancient paths," by believing various ideas and secular concepts which are not biblical (Jeremiah 18:15). Lives are being diminished by disobedience, and it truly breaks our Father's heart.

Many women are walking in darkness. In order to dispel the darkness, we need to turn on the light. God has told us that His Word will light our path (Psalm 119:105). The goal of this study is to discern God's will for women as we learn what Scripture reveals about women of the Word.

As a young mother in the 1970's, I encountered scores of good Bible studies dealing with being a woman of God. Today there are only a few to be found, yet there is an increasingly dire need for teaching biblical mandates for women.

Through the strong and helpful encouragement of my husband, Dave, and the enthusiastic support of our five children, the Lord led me in preparing this material. Special thanks to the many women who have continually encouraged me, and to Dave who has spent countless hours formatting these materials.

While preparing this study I learned much, and the Lord has used His Word to exhort and challenge me to personal spiritual growth. My prayer is that as you dig into the Word, you will become conformed to the image of Christ.

"For I am confident of this very thing, that He who began a good work in you will perfect it until the day of Christ Jesus. For it is only right for me to feel this way about you all, because I have you in my heart..."
Philippians 1:6,7a

Judy

How to Use this Study

During this study we will focus on God's specific directives for women. Taking biblical commands and precepts one by one, our goal will be to determine what God is telling us to do, and to explore how they are practical for the "nitty-gritty" of daily living.

How do women of the Word go about living in this world today? *Ancient Paths for Modern Women* is a four-part discipleship program designed to be most effective when studied in sequence.

- **Ancient Paths I- Walking With the Lord** (seven weeks), addresses how to develop an intimate, personal walk with the Lord.

- **Ancient Paths II- Walking as Wives** (seven weeks), leads us to learn and apply what God says about women walking as wives in the marriage relationship.

- **Ancient Paths III- Walking as Mothers and Homemakers** (seven weeks), examines the Lord's desire for women as they disciple their children and build God-honoring homes.

- **Ancient Paths IV- Walking in the Church and in the World** (eight weeks), grapples with issues related to God's will for women in the church, a woman's walk in the secular world, and how to keep walking faithfully.

It is preferable to have each chapter's work completed prior to the Bible study time. Many chapters have questions marked "***Optional.**" If you choose to answer those questions, you will need additional Bible study resource books. A description of these is located at the back of this study.

You will notice that each page has a "Prayer Points" area provided in the margin. This is designed for use in jotting down ideas, items for discussion, questions, group prayer requests, or personal prayer needs that the Holy Spirit may bring to mind during the study.

The last page of each chapter is best handled in a small group format. It is recommended that you complete and record your "Summary," "Discussion" and "Application" responses prior to the lesson so that you can share your answers and ideas.

It is suggested that you use the chapter heading as a type of filing system. It may be a notebook with pockets or a portable file. As time goes by, insert current events, magazine articles, and even cartoons into the appropriate chapter topic. Be alert for other applicable Scripture to insert in various chapters. The long-term goal is that you will be able to teach and encourage other women as you mature in the Lord using the enclosed materials.

⌘ ⌘ ⌘

Ancient Paths Bible Study Series is especially effective when used by "older women" as they mentor "younger women." The long-term goal of this study is that you will be able to teach and encourage other women as you both mature in the Lord.

"Come, Walk the Ancient Paths"

Come and walk the ancient paths	[Jeremiah 6:16]
That lead into the Savior's heart.	[Revelation 19:7]
His Word reveals the wisdom past	[Proverbs 4:11]
Of just one Way to life and rest,	[John 14:6]
So choose this route and start.	[Deuteronomy 30:19]
Come, walk the road that leads to joy,	[Psalm 16:11]
And though the trail may steepen,	[James 1:2]
The obstacles of Satan's ploys	[Ephesians 6:10-13]
Thrust us on Jesus to employ	[II Corinthians12:9, 10]
His grace, which daily deepens.	[Hebrews 4:16]
Come, run by grace, the ancient race,	[Hebrews 12:1]
Intent to win the prize.	[I Corinthians 9:24]
The goal in view is Jesus' face;	[Hebrews 12:1]
Press on, reach out, pick up the pace	[Philippians 3:13, 14]
Toward heaven set your eyes.	[Hebrews 12:2]
Then stand before the Bema Seat	[II Corinthians 5:10]
Rewarded by the Son.	[II Timothy 4:8]
To place our crowns back at His feet	[Revelation 4:10]
Will be our joy. Our prize most sweet	[Philippians 4:1]
To hear Him say, "Well done."	[Matthew 25:21]
Be seated in the heavenly places	[Ephesians 2:6]
With Christ, forever home.	[Revelation 21:3]
Our walk by faith, and zeal of race,	[II Corinthians 5:6, 7]
Will show the riches of His grace	[II Timothy 4:7]
In ages yet to come.	[Ephesians 2:7]
Come, walk the ancient paths.	[Jeremiah 6:16]

Judy Gerry

Becoming a Follower of Christ

1. Recognize that God loves you:

"For God so loved the world that He gave His one and only Son, that whoever believes in Him shall not perish but have eternal life." (John 3:16)

"But God demonstrates His own love for us in this: While we were still sinners, Christ died for us." (Romans 5:8)

2. Admit that you are a sinner:

"For all have sinned and fall short of the glory of God." (Romans 3:23)

"As it is written: 'There is no one righteous, not even one.'" (Romans 3:10)

3. Recognize Jesus Christ as being God's only remedy for sin:

"For the wages of sin is death, but the gift of God is eternal life in Christ Jesus our Lord." (Romans 6:23)

"Yet all who received Him, to those who believed in His name, He gave the right to become children of God." (John 1:12)

"For what I received I passed on to you as of first importance: that Christ died for our sins according to the Scriptures, that He was buried, that He was raised on the third day according to the Scriptures." (I Corinthians 15:3, 4)

4. Receive Jesus Christ as your personal Savior:

"If you confess with your mouth, 'Jesus is Lord,' and believe in your heart that God raised Him from the dead, you will be saved." (Romans 10:9)

Prayer is simply "talking with God." Right now, go to God in prayer and ask Christ to be your Savior. You might pray something like this:

"Lord Jesus, I need You. I confess that I am a sinner and that You paid the penalty for my sin through Your death on the cross. I believe that You died for my sins and were raised from the dead. I ask You to come into my heart, take control of my life, and make me the kind of person that You want me to be. Thank You for coming into my life as You promised. Amen."

WALKING AS WIVES

"I will walk within my house in the integrity of my heart."
Psalm 101:2

Before We Begin...
Marriage and the home are God's idea. In the coming weeks we will be studying the husband-wife relationship. God's Word is filled with instruction for married women.

Regarding those who have not yet met Christ as their Savior:
Some of you may not yet know Jesus Christ as your personal Savior. This Bible study will be beneficial because anytime that God's principles are applied to our lives there will always be a positive result. However, we will never experience God's best in our marriages until we meet Him personally in our own individual lives.

If you have not yet made the wonderful discovery of knowing Christ, please take time to carefully read the preceding page; "Becoming a Follower of Christ." Attempts to live the Christian life without having His power in your life will end in frustration. If you want to experience the abundant life that the Lord has created you to enjoy, before you begin this Bible study, begin to follow Jesus.

Regarding those who are not married:
Some taking this study may not be married. There are multitudes of single women whose lives are a "fragrant aroma" to God. As we walk with the Lord, He will fulfill His purposes in our lives whether we are married or single; being in God's will is what matters, not our marital status. Will the following studies dealing with "Walking as Wives" relate to singles? Absolutely!

Those women who are currently single are a vital part of God's plan. Perhaps you will marry in the future; these next chapters will help to equip you to recognize a godly man, and they will prepare you for being a godly wife.

Perhaps you may remain single; that, too, is part of God's perfect plan for your life (I Corinthians 7:7, 8). Paul tells us that single women have even more opportunity for service to offer in the church than their married counterparts (I Corinthians 7:25-38). The Lord wants to use you single women in the lives of all other believers! Single women are in a unique position to be a great source of encouragement and strength to all of the women within the church. The following chapters will enable you to minister more effectively in the church, as you understand God's specific plans for your married sisters in the Lord.

As we study "Walking as Wives," open sharing and interaction among women from all walks of life will be essential and valuable. Regardless of our unique, personal circumstances, every woman is a precious creation; a treasure to God Himself (Psalm 83:3). All of God's Word is for all of us. We need each other; so let's get started!

CHAPTER ONE

BE SENSIBLE

Refusing to dwell on thoughts that don't honor God.

"Encourage the young women ... to be sensible... "
Titus 2:4, 5

" I will walk within my house in the integrity of my heart.."
Psalm 101:2

" I will walk within my house in the integrity of my heart.."
Psalm 101:2

Prayer Points:

As we begin our study of God's instructions to women regarding walking in our homes, let us first look at King David's words penned three thousand years ago.

David was committed to walking in his home with a heart of innocence and integrity. Integrity means completeness, wholeness. He was committed to living in such a way that the person he was in one part of life was the same person he was in every other arena of his life. David was committed to consistently integrating his walk with the Lord with his walk in his home.

In other words, he did not want to be a hypocrite at home.

Many women, as well as men, have trouble integrating their "church talk" with their "home walk." Many marriages have suffered ruin, and many children have rebelled from following the Lord, because wives and mothers have not applied God's Word to their home lives.

Some sincere women have not walked within their house in the integrity of their hearts because they have been ignorant of what God's specific instruction has been for them.

Some women have failed because they have chosen either intentionally, or through passive neglect, to disobey what they knew to be true in God's Word regarding their home lives.

Regardless of the reason for failing to obey God's Word, disobedience is sin. As believers, we have the unique privilege and responsibility to walk in God's ways to please Him. Of all women on earth, we have the rare opportunity to experience God's spectacular blessing as we study and apply His Word to our lives;

Reading it in ...
Writing it down ...
Praying it up ...
and Living it out.

The Lord has told us specific things related to the way in which women are to conduct themselves in their homes. Our walk at home flows directly out of our walk with Him. A changed relationship with our Creator affects every other area of our life.

Prayer Points:

Godly thinking leads to godly behavior. As we begin to examine the husband-wife relationship, we must realize that the way that we interact with our husband is actually a byproduct of the thoughts and beliefs that we have regarding marriage. We must begin by getting our thoughts in line with God's thoughts. We must learn to be sensible.

The Greek word for sensible, "sophron," is used as an admonition for young women in the church. It reflects a high biblical standard for women since this term is also used in describing the qualifications for church elders [Titus 1:8; I Timothy 3:2], and in describing mature men [Titus 2:2].

Webster's New World College Dictionary defines 'sensible' this way:

a) that which can cause physical sensation; perceptible to the senses
b) perceptible to the intellect
c) easily perceived; marked; striking; appreciable
d) having senses; capable of receiving sensation; sensitive
e) having appreciation or understanding; emotionally or intellectually aware (sensible of another's grief)
f) having or showing good sense or sound judgment; intelligent; reasonable; wise.

In Scripture, the word sensible means being of sound mind, self-controlled, disciplined, or sober minded. It is occasionally used interchangeably with the word prudence. The term discretion is also found in the King James Version for "sophron."

"Sophron" is comprised of two Greek words: "sozo," meaning "to save," and "phren," meaning "the mind." When we are "sensible," we are literally "saving the mind." To be sensible is the opposite of "losing your mind," or of being impulsively "out of your mind."

To be sensible means to possess sound judgment which, coupled with an inner strength, enables us to live in a way that is pleasing to God. Sensibility is that quality which allows one to control his passions and desires. It is mental "self-control" and discipline that encourages reasonable, logical thought [Isaiah 1:18].

When faced with how to respond to life circumstances, many people believe that "going with their gut feeling" will lead them into God's will. They assume that sound judgment, and sensibility, is simply a function of "common sense."

What do the following verses indicate about man's natural thought processes?

1. Isaiah 55:8, 9

2. II Corinthians 4:3, 4

3. I Corinthians 2:14

Rather than relying on common sense, contemporary wisdom, or natural impulse, God tells us that we should not "conform any longer to the pattern of this world." We are to be "transformed by the renewing of your mind. Then you will be able to test and approve what God's will is – His good, pleasing and perfect will" (Romans 12:2). Our minds need to be renewed continually. It is a daily discipline and ongoing process throughout our lives.

But, is it really possible to change our thought processes? How can our minds be renewed? How can we begin to use sound judgment that is in harmony with the thoughts and will of God?

What do you learn about the origin of a sound mind or mental self-control in the following verses?

4. II Timothy 1:7

5. James 1:5 How do we get wisdom?

6. Galatians 5:23

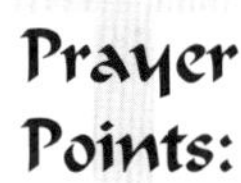

Prayer Points:

7. I Corinthians 2:15, 16

What does a spiritual man do?

What mind does the spiritual man possess?

We know that the Lord is the giver of "sophron." He lives it out in our lives through the power of the Holy Spirit. God tells us that we actually possess the mind of Christ! With that being true, why is it that we continue to struggle with thought patterns that are not in harmony with God's thoughts?

Does the Lord give some believers more "sophron" than others? Why is it that certain people have better judgment and know what direction is the right way to go (I Chronicles 12:32)? Do we have anything to do with this quality of sensibility in our lives?

What do the following verses indicate about our personal responsibility in being sensible and mentally self-disciplined?

8. II Peter 1:5, 6

9. II Corinthians 10:5

Prayer Points:

[*note: for added study regarding our thought life, review the "Quiet Spirit" in *Ancient Paths I*, Chapter 5.]

10. I Thessalonians 5:21-23

Though we may intellectually agree that being sensible is a noble goal, our feelings often militate against the sensibility that has been given to us by the Lord. Are there times in your life when your mind tells you the proper course of action to take; yet your emotions tell you to forget it?

There is a common notion that a woman is not always responsible for how she feels and that she is controlled by those feelings. Some women even use mood swings as excuses for not exercising a sensible and controlled spirit.

Do you occasionally, or even frequently, find yourself "reacting" to life rather than "responding" appropriately to circumstances? Emotions are a gift from God. The mature woman definitely has feelings, but she has learned to master those feelings rather than to be mastered by them (I Corinthians 6:12).

We are created as emotional beings. Emotions are a gift from God. They are not wrong; it is what we do with those feelings that result in either good or evil. Sometimes depression, or "the blahs," can sneak into our lives undetected until we are almost overwhelmed by the emotion.

Though Christian women are given a sound mind from the Lord, there are inevitable times when we don't feel like following sensible judgments. Many of us think that we handle the emotional ups and downs of life quite successfully. Yet, if we were to ask our family members how they perceive our success in handling our emotions, their answers might surprise us.

We must learn to understand our emotions, control them, and express them properly. We must act on what God says, whether we feel like it or not.

Prayer Points:

11. Psalm 43

When the psalmist wrote this, he was in exile north of Israel. In the first two verses he talks to God about his "feelings." How would you describe the emotional condition of the writer in these verses?

In verses 3 and 4, the writer begins to shift his focus away from his circumstances. Upon what does the psalmist concentrate?

In verse 5, would you say that the psalmist "listens to himself," or would you say that he "instructs himself?"

What advice does he give?

What might this tell you about how to handle typical depression?

The psalmist did not deny his despair, but he refocused on the hope that God offers. It has been said that when darkness envelops us, "we should not attack the darkness; rather, we should turn on the light." In order to make sound judgments during times of darkness, we must keep focusing on Christ Who is the Light of the world (John 8:12), and on His word which is a light to our path (Psalm 119:105).

Following are Scriptures that give us two accounts of individuals who refused to be sensible.

12. Luke 15:11-24

What words would you use to describe the attitude and actions of the son in verses 11-16?

What words would you use to describe the attitude and actions of the son in verses 18-21?

What turning point occurred in verse 17 that changed the direction of this son's life?

When we refuse to be sensible, our attitudes and actions are dictated by self-gratification. When we refuse to use sound judgment, we fail to discern the destructive nature of our natural impulses. Lacking sober-mindedness, we succumb to the intoxicating greed and lust that can lead us into hurtful places where we never intended to go.

The wonderful news is that, like the younger son, it is never too late to repent! Our own Father feels compassion for us (Isaiah 30:18). He is watchfully waiting for us to return. When we "come back to our senses," our Father runs toward us, embraces us, kisses us, and restores us. He doesn't chide us, He celebrates our reunion (Luke 11:22-24).

13. Daniel 4:28-37

What words would you use to describe the attitude and actions of the king in verses 28-33?

What words would you use to describe the attitude and actions of the king in verses 34-37?

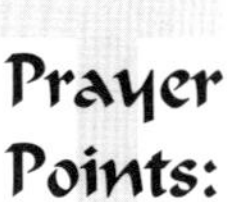

Prayer Points:

What turning point occurred in verse 34 that changed the direction of the king's life?

When the prodigal son and King Nebuchadnezzer returned to their senses, they began to perceive a more accurate view of God. They also began to see their lives from God's point of view. Our Father's desire is that we experience intimacy with Him. He wants the best in our lives. The path of obedience always leads to experiencing His blessing and joy (John 13:17).

God desires that women be sensible. What are some tangible benefits of being sensible, discreet, or prudent?

14. Proverbs 2:11

15. Proverbs 27:12

If possible, recount a time when you "proceeded and had to pay the penalty."

What did you learn from that experience?

Can you identify any specific area(s) of weakness in your own life where you tend not to use sound judgment?

Prayer Points:

Optional: Look up the Hebrew word used in Proverbs 27:12 to describe the person who lacks sensibility. What does this tell you about being "open-minded?"

To become sensible is a decision that needs to be continually renewed. As believers, we have been given the mind of Christ. He is speaking to us. We must discipline our minds to listen to His quiet voice (I Kings 19:12). As we take our thoughts captive and listen to the Lord, "whether you turn to the right or to the left, your ears will hear a voice behind you, saying, 'This is the way; walk in it'" (Isaiah 30:21NIV).

There are voices crying for attention all around us. The world seduces us with its siren song, our own flesh calls to us demanding satisfaction; we are tempted at every turn to go the wrong way. How are we to discern the voice of the Lord from all of the other cries?

We must discipline our minds to listen only to Him. God will never tell us to do anything that is contrary to what He has already revealed through His written Word. In order to be "noble-minded," we must examine the Scriptures daily to see whether these things are so" (Acts 17:11). We can know that our thoughts are in line with His thoughts when they measure up to the plumb line of the Bible.

16. Read II Timothy 3:16

How might God's Word help us to become sensible?

17. Read Hebrews 5:11-14

How are the "listening skills" of God's people described in verse 11?

Prayer Points:

According to this passage, how do believers become spiritually mature and "train themselves to distinguish good from evil?"

In light of this passage, what practical steps might you practice in your own life in order to develop sound judgment and sensibility?

In the coming weeks as we examine the husband-wife relationship, we must be willing to have our thoughts aligned with God's thoughts. Are you willing to cooperate with the Lord as He tells you, "this is the way; walk in it?"

Becoming sensible is a process. It is a work of the Holy Spirit in our lives as we have the mind of Christ. Being sensible requires our training and practice. It also sets the stage for God to do more in our lives than we can even dream possible (I Corinthians 9:11).

Take a moment and consider the quality of "being sensible" in your own life.

- Would you say that you are generally known as a woman who is sensible (able to make sound judgments)?

If you answered "yes," what factors in your life have most influenced your developing the quality of being sensible?

- Do you need to repent of any areas in which you have refused to be sensible?

As we begin to study God's thoughts on marriage, yield yourself to the Lord, and ask Him to accomplish His purposes in your home and life as He transforms you by the renewing of your mind (Romans 12:1, 2).

Prayer Points:

SUMMARY:

Define "sensible" in your own terms. You could use a synonym, a motto, a poem or a prayer, or even make a drawing to show your understanding of this quality.

DISCUSSION:

What kinds of things in today's culture tend to work against a woman developing the biblical quality of being sensible?

APPLICATION:

Your Christian friend habitually makes her decisions based upon what seems to "feel right" at the moment. Her decisions continually get her into trouble. She asks you why it is that things keep going wrong in her life. What do you say?

CHAPTER TWO

BE TEMPERATE

Exercising the self-control that is necessary to do what I know is right.

"Women must likewise be... temperate..."
I Timothy 3:11

"Women must likewise be... temperate..."
I Timothy 3:11

Prayer Points:

The Lord greatly values the quality of being temperate, and He mentions it in conjunction with women in the Word. Not only are older men (Titus 2:2) and elders instructed to be temperate (I Timothy 3:2), Paul also instructs the wives of men who serve in any way in the church to be temperate (I Timothy 3:11).

Webster's New World College Dictionary defines 'temperate' this way:

a) *moderate in indulging the appetites; not self-indulgent; abstemious, especially in the use of alcoholic liquors*
b) *moderate in one's actions, speech, etc; self-restrained*
c) *moderate or restrained (a temperate reply)*
d) *neither very hot nor very cold (said of climate, etc.)*

While being sensible relates to having the inner strength of mental discipline and sound judgment, being temperate relates to having the self-discipline to make obedient actions a reality.

The biblical translation of the Greek word for temperate is "sober." It implies control over one's appetites and passions with the goal of not exceeding the bounds of what is right or proper.

The opposite concept of being temperate is to be unrestrained, frivolous, flippant, or excessive in actions. God's will is for women not to be self-indulgent, but to be self-restrained and moderate in all that we do. His Word stresses the importance of being temperate.

1. Proverbs 25:28

   What do you think the writer means by the term, "a city that is broken into and without walls?"

We have seen previously that self-control is the fruit of the Spirit (Galatians 5:23). Yet we also have seen that self-control is a quality which takes effort on our part.

There is a mysterious connection between the quality of being temperate and the condition of our soul. The soul is the seat of our mind, emotion, intellect and will. What do the following verses reveal about this linkage?

Prayer Points:

2. James 1:14, 15

3. I Peter 2:11

God always wants the best for us so He has given us His Word in order to direct us and protect us. Because we are indwelt by the Holy Spirit, we can choose to be temperate or not.

4. I Corinthians 6:12.

   Why does Paul choose to exercise temperance in his life?

5. Read Romans 6:14.

   What should not have mastery over believers?

Scripture teaches that before we were saved we were powerless to stop sinning; we were "slaves of sin" (Romans 6:17). But, after salvation we were set free. As Christians, we have the power to choose whether to sin or not.

6. I Corinthians 9:25-27

   How does Paul develop temperance?

Why does he do this?

Prayer Points:

Are there any areas of your physical life that need to be "buffeted?"

Why would it be important for you to "buffet" your body in this area?

Optional: Look up the word for "buffet" found in I Corinthians 9:27. What insights can you gain from this definition about the seriousness, and manner, of godly personal discipline?

The Lord exhorts us to, "discipline yourself for the purpose of godliness; for bodily discipline is only of little profit, but godliness is profitable for all things, since it holds promise for the present life and also for the life to come" (I Timothy 4:7, 8).

The Lord does not tell us in His Word to discipline ourselves and avoid certain things because He wants us to miss out on all the fun in life. As a matter of fact, He tells us that the abundant and full life are found in Christ (John 10:10), and that wherever He is, is precisely the place where we will find fullness of joy and true pleasure (Psalm 16:11).

We are warned to control ourselves from certain practices and activities because they are harmful to us. Much like a mother warns her child to avoid dangerous situations, God warns us through His Word. His motivation is His great love for us.

The Lord exhorts those whom He loves to become temperate. Prior to Abel's murder, God warned Cain that "sin is crouching at the door; and its desire is for you, but you must master it" (Genesis 4:7). Cain should have heeded God's warning. We should heed God's warnings today.

It has been said that, "the measure of a woman is not in what she possesses, but in what possesses her." What is it that holds us, restrains us, compels us, or motivates us?

Is there some sin in your life over which you seem to have no control? Have you ever heard yourself say, "I just can't help doing (fill in the blank)?" In your marriage, do you ever excuse wrong attitudes or behaviors by saying, "My husband will just have to accept it because that's just the way that I am?"

Perhaps you find yourself saying, "I've tried to stop (fill in the blank), but it's no use"? It is easier to admit that we have a "weak area" than it is to admit that we are "slaves" to a certain undesirable activity.

7. II Peter 2:19b

   Identify one area of habitual "weakness" in your life where you seem to always "lose the battle."

   In light of this verse, if your "weak area" has overcome your sensible will, what does that make you?

   How does that make you feel?

We do not have to be prisoners of our passions, or captives of our impulsive natures. We can make the choice to listen to sensible thinking, and behave in temperate ways.

8. Matthew 26:35-45

Would you say that Peter's thoughts in verse 35 were sensible and God-honoring?

What did Jesus ask Peter to do?

Peter wanted to be faithful in his actions; was he successful in accomplishing what he hoped to do?

What do you learn in verse 41 that might help you to develop temperance in your life?

Temperance is action-oriented. When God uses the term temperate in Scripture, it is used particularly in reference to abstaining from much wine. There are women who struggle in this area, but any area of our lives can become a problem if we fail to be temperate women.

We make a mistake if we assume that the object of our intemperance is the actual sin itself. When Peter failed to control his actions, "sleep" was not the culprit. Scripture tells us that sleeping is a gift from the Lord (Psalm 127:2), and yet, even sleep can be abused (Proverbs 6:9-11). "Every good and perfect gift is from above, coming down from the Father" (James 1:17). Everything that God has given to us is good (Romans 14:14).

It is our lack of moderation, self-control, and self indulgence which God sees as sin.

Physical intemperance wages war against our soul (I Peter 2:11). Each time that we choose to become a slave to sin, the "walls of our city" are broken down (Proverbs 25:28) and we are weakened for the next ensuing battle. Three times in a row, Peter surrendered his sound judgment in response to his body's demand for immediate sleep. It was only hours later that he found himself denying Christ three times in a row (Matthew 26:69-75). Peter started out with noble thoughts and aspirations, yet, he failed to exercise temperance.

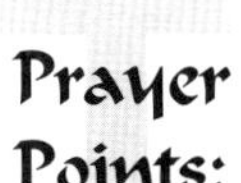

While it may be easy to discern certain areas in other's lives where self-control is lacking, it may be more difficult to address a lack of temperance in our own lives. Intemperance takes on many forms.

Read each verse below. In what specific areas of life are we exhorted to exhibit temperance, moderation, or sobriety?

9. Proverbs 23:19-21

10. I Corinthians 10:31

11. Hebrews 13:5

12. Hebrews 13:4

13. I Thessalonians 4:3-5

14. I Timothy 2:9, 10

15. I Peter 3:3, 4

16. Proverbs 15:1, 2

Prayer Points:

17. Proverbs 16:32

18. Proverbs 6:9-11

It is one thing to be mentally sensible and know what one should do; it is altogether another thing to be temperate by taking action and putting those thoughts into practice. As wives, we may come up with myriads of excuses as to why we cannot obey God in a given area of our marriage. Yet, if we refuse to take action on what God tells us to do in His Word, we must conclude two things about ourselves:

- ***Our faith in God is not strong (James 2:17).***
- ***Our love for the Lord is weak (John 14:21a).***

On the other hand, if we obediently take action when the Lord instructs us, we can anticipate many things:

- ***Our joy will be made full (John 15:11).***
- ***We will be fruitful in our homes (Psalm 128:3).***
- ***Our households will be built up (Proverbs 14:1).***
- ***We will experience the blessing and joy of a growing love-relationship with the Lord (John 14:21b).***

As we begin looking at specific instructions for marriage, we must start by examining ourselves before God.

19. Would you say that you are a temperate woman (able to control your desires and to put sound judgments into practice)?

Would your husband say that you are a temperate woman?

If the Holy Spirit has shown you that there is an area of intemperance in your life;

Prayer Points:

a) ***immediately confess that as sin,***

b) ***thank Him for forgiving you,***

c) ***ask Christ to give you the grace and power to be victorious in this area,***

d) ***ask the Lord to show you certain steps to begin today in a new direction of moderation and self-control.***

e) ***then, OBEY the Lord!***

As believing women, we have been given the choice by God to choose what it is that we will serve and obey. In the coming chapters we will be examining God's will for women in the marriage relationship. Is it your commitment to exercise temperance in your life as the Lord reveals His will for your life?

Are you willing to obey Him as He instructs you regarding His will for your marriage? If so, tell Him now.

In the space below, write a letter to the Lord expressing your desire to become a woman who is temperate in every area of her life.

"Keep watching and praying that you may not enter into temptation; the spirit is willing, but the flesh is weak."
Matthew 26:41

Prayer Points:

SUMMARY:

Define "temperate" in your own terms. You could use a synonym, a motto, a poem or a prayer, or even make a drawing to show your understanding of this quality.

DISCUSSION:

Do you think that it is possible for a woman to be sensible without being temperate?

Is it possible for her to be temperate without being sensible?

APPLICATION:

Your Christian friend is a compulsive shopper. Seeing a sale advertisement can send her into a frenzy. Even though her husband is complaining about their debts, and every closet in her house is full of clothes, she keeps buying more. Can you give her any advice to help her become temperate in this area?

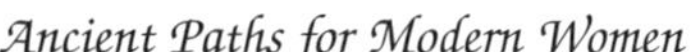

CHAPTER THREE

LOVE YOUR HUSBAND

Nurturing a tender affection and friendship with my husband.

"... so that they (older women) may encourage the young women to love their husbands."
Titus 2:3-4

"This is my lover, this is my friend..."
Song of Solomon 5:16 (NIV)

Prayer Points:

" ...so that they (older women) may encourage the young women to love their husbands." Titus 2:3-4

"This is my lover, this is my friend..." Song of Solomon 5:16 NIV

A bride on her wedding day cannot imagine needing to learn to love her groom. The love that she has for him is what brings her to the altar, committing her life to him. In our Western culture, the elements of emotional, romantic love combined with common interests usually provide the basis for marriage.

Yet, we see in God's Word that older women are to encourage and to train younger women to love their husbands. The word used for "train" implies that learning to love our husbands is a process requiring time and effort.

Without investing the time and effort required in order to learn to love our husbands, the "glow" of the bride on her wedding day can become a "glower" with passing years. The "marital arts" in which we are to be trained may become distorted into something more akin to "martial arts," and rather than "completing each other" couples may actually begin "competing with each other."

Today, many marriages are growing cold and disintegrating because husbands and wives have failed to love each other God's way.

Marriage was designed to be a blessing from the Lord (Proverbs 18:22; 19:14). God created male and female (Matthew 19:4) and He intended that "the two should become one" (Ephesians 5:31). In marriage, neither sex is independent of the other; rather, they are interdependent, According to I Corinthians 11:11, 12:

"However, in the Lord, neither is woman independent of man, nor is man independent of woman. For as the woman originates from the man, so also the man has his birth through the woman; and all things originate from God."

There are many Scriptural commands for husbands to love their wives using the term "agapao" or "agape" (Ephesians 5:25, Colossians 3:19). This love is the type that does the right thing regardless of feelings.

"Agapao" love is best exhibited by Christ when He came to earth to die for our sin. It is self-sacrificing. He did not desire emotionally to die on the cross that day, but His will was to do the will of the Father (Matthew 26:38, 39).

Prayer Points:

This model of love is the example of how all believers are commanded to love. God does not command us to love because we feel like it; rather, He directs us to think, speak and act in a loving manner (I John 3:23). To love when we do not feel like it is simply a matter of faithful obedience (John 14:15), and is a response to the love that God has for us (I John 4:10, 11, 19).

Husbands are particularly commanded to love their wives with "agape" love because his love is a picture of Christ's love for His bride, the church. Additionally, husbands are exhorted to exhibit a second type of love toward their wives; "phileo" love (I Peter 3:7).

Though all believers are to have agape love for each other, the only biblical passage where wives are specifically exhorted to "love their husbands" uses the term "phileo" love (Titus 2:4). "Phileo" love is the special type of love that wives are to learn to demonstrate toward their husbands.

The English language is limited in describing the nuances of the word "love." The Greek language of the New Testament has many words that are all translated "love" in English. What is it about the quality of "phileo" that causes it to be uniquely singled out as the type of love that wives are to learn to exhibit toward their husbands?

What is "phileo?"

a) Phileo *is emotional in nature and cannot be commanded, but can be developed. It is a tender affection.*

b) Phileo *is a selective love, based on the qualities in another person that one finds admirable, attractive and appealing.*

c) Phileo *is fellowship love requiring enjoyable interaction through comradeship and communication. (example: "two souls knit together" - I Samuel 18:1)*

Prayer Points:

d) Phileo *is the living relationship between two friends that will wither if it is not consistently growing and being nurtured.*

e) Phileo *makes dear friends who share in each other's thoughts, feelings, attitudes, plans and dreams – the most intimate things they could share with few others.*

f) Phileo *feels and expresses delight in its actions toward the other person.*

Basically, when God instructs a wife to "phileo" her husband, He is exhorting her to become her husband's intimate friend.

Many marriages have romance ("eros") and even have self-sacrificing commitment ("agapao") but lack a sense of oneness and true friendship. As women of the Word, we need to learn to cherish and to become cherished; we need to learn to be a companion, we need to learn to be a "phileo" friend.

Webster's New World College Dictionary defines "friend" this way:

a) a person whom one knows well and is fond of; intimate associate; close acquaintance
b) a person on the same side in a struggle; one who is not an enemy or foe; ally
c) a support or sympathizer (a friend of labor)
d) something thought of as like a friend in being helpful, reliable, etc.

If women are going to love and intimately support their husbands as friends, it is necessary that they understand their husband's needs. Let's begin by examining God's initial design for the husband-wife marital relationship. Though Adam and Eve were unique individuals, their lives serve as an example, and have a continuing effect, on our lives today (Romans 5:12-14; I Timothy 2:11-14).

1. Genesis 2:18-20

Until this point in creation God had called everything "good." What did He call "not good?"

What did God do to solve the problem?

Adam needed a companion and God specially provided Eve.

Your husband needs a companion also, and God has uniquely provided you in his life. Consider your husband's life; identify those times when he is "alone."

Prayer Points:

As you consider areas where your husband is "alone," have you made an effort to occasionally come alongside him and share that experience?

- Do you cheerfully go with your husband to sports events that HE likes ... just so that you can be with him?
- Do you make yourself available to accompany your husband to stores where HE likes to shop? (hardware, sports equipment, computer stores, auto supply stores, etc.)
- Have you learned to appreciate the type of entertainment that HE prefers – just so that you can be with him?
- When your husband is working on a home project, do you often make a point of coming alongside to cheer him on?
- Do you express sincere interest in how your husband spends his days at work?
- Do you occasionally perceive that your husband might be lonely for your presence? If your husband has invited you to join him in one of his activities, and you have declined his invitation a few times, he will most likely stop asking you to accompany him. Can you think of any area of your husband's life where you might have given him the impression that you prefer not to join him?

While every individual needs and enjoys private time, many wives miss opportunities to nurture their relationship with their husband by neglecting to join him in his activities. "It is not good for the man to be alone." Many husbands are lonely.

It has been sadly said, "Behind every great man there is a woman who encourages and appreciates him; unfortunately, it's not always his wife."

Prayer Points:

- Do you ever perceive that your husband might be lonely for you to participate emotionally, or intellectually, with him in his career? If your husband has initiated conversation related to his work activities, or regarding his coworkers, and you have expressed even mild disinterest, he will most likely stop trying to include you in this area of his life. Have you ever given him the impression that you are not interested in his occupational activities?

Every woman longs to sense that she is understood and is valuable. Yet, we often forget that this is also a deep need in men. Realizing that it takes training and practice, how do we go about learning to exhibit true "phileo" to our husbands?

2. Titus 2:3, 4

Who is commanded to train the younger women in "phileo-ing," (not "filleting"), their husbands?

Do you sense that the church today is successful in fulfilling this function?

If you are one of the "older women," how are you obeying this admonition?

Older women often shy away from their God-given roles because they feel as though their wisdom and experience is not needed. If you are one of the "younger women," how have you made yourself teachable and open to an "older woman?"

3. Titus 3:4, 5

The love discussed in these verses is "phileo" love. How was God's "phileo" love for mankind demonstrated?

Did anyone request of the Father that He demonstrate this "phileo" love?

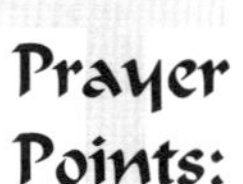

Prayer Points:

Had the recipients of God's "phileo" done anything to earn His kind act of love?

What might this tell you about the way that you are to demonstrate "phileo" love to your husband?

Consider ways in which you can demonstrate this type of "phileo" love to your husband. Begin by asking yourself these questions:

- Have I sacrificed my own schedule in order to facilitate his timetable?
- Have I chosen to subjugate my own preferences in our selection of TV shows, what we do with our free time, or how we invest our resources, in order to meet his unspoken desires?
- Have I anticipated his unspoken needs ahead of time in order to meet them?
- Without being asked, have I sacrificed my plans in order to make him successful in his endeavors?

In the space below, give one specific example of a kind, unsolicited demonstration of your love that you have recently shown your husband. (This act of love may have even gone unnoticed by your husband.)

Prayer Points:

A wife who loves her husband with "phileo" love will be looking for ways to demonstrate it. Just as Christ demonstrated His friendship with us (John 15:15) by sacrificing Himself on our behalf (Titus 3:4, 5), Jesus tells us that the greatest love is shown when a person "lay(s) down his life for his friends" (John 15:13). A wife demonstrating "phileo" love will try to anticipate, and sacrificially meet, her husband's needs before he even becomes aware of them.

4. Acts 28:2

What specific acts of "phileo" love did the natives show to Paul and those shipwrecked?

Why did the natives do this for them?

What does this tell you about the way that you are to demonstrate "phileo" love to your husband?

Consider ways in which you can demonstrate this type of "phileo" love to your husband. Begin by asking yourself these questions:

- Have I made sure that the clothing he requires is clean and ready to be worn?
- Have I organized our home so that my husband has a comfortable place to sit and relax?
- Do I consistently prepare nourishing meals that HE likes?
- Is our home orderly, warm, and welcoming for my husband?

Give one specific example of a kind, physical demonstration of "phileo" love that you have recently shown your husband.

A wife who loves her husband with "phileo" love will be aware of her husband's current physical needs. During demanding times she will be there eagerly warming, comforting, and nurturing her husband.

Prayer Points:

5. John 5:20a

   How does the Father demonstrate His "phileo" love for His Son?

   What does this tell you about the way that you are to demonstrate "phileo" to your husband?

Consider ways in which you can demonstrate this type of "phileo" love to your husband. Begin by asking yourself these questions:

- When my husband talks with me, do I stop what I am doing and make eye contact with him?
- When I have important news to share, do I tell my husband first, or do I often share the news with others before telling him?
- Do I openly communicate with my husband, or do I keep some things secret from him?
- Have I freely shared with my husband the hopes, dreams, and aspirations that I have?
- Is my husband aware of the way that I spend my time each day?

  In the space below, write out any changes that you, personally, need to make in the way that you communicate with your husband.

A wife who loves her husband with "phileo" love will eagerly seek opportunities to communicate with her husband. She desires to know the heart of her husband, and to have him know hers.

6. Song of Solomon 5:16b

Solomon's bride refers to her husband using what two endearing terms?

Do you think that these two terms differ from each other? If so, how?

If you were describing your relationship with your husband, would both of these terms accurately capture the tone of your marriage? If not, why not?

Optional: Read I Corinthians 13. What Greek word for "love" is used in this text? Do you think that this chapter is applicable to the marriage relationship? Why, or why not? Take some time to paraphrase this chapter, personalizing it to reflect what this type of love would look like when demonstrated in your own home.

7. Proverbs 31:10-12

How valuable is an "excellent wife?"

What is her relationship like with her husband?

8. Proverbs 12:4

How do your actions and attitudes affect your husband's life?

Becoming the intimate friend and soul-mate of your husband requires training and practice. What do the following verses reveal regarding specific ways that a wife can show "phileo" love to her husband-friend?

Prayer Points:

9. Proverbs 27:17

10. Luke 14:10

What does Scripture warn against that might hinder building true friendship in relationships?

11. Proverbs 16:28

    When talking with others, do you always speak of your husband in a positive light; never mocking, ridiculing, or accusing him?

    Are you guilty of revealing intimate secrets to others that should be held in confidence between you and your husband?

    When speaking with your children, are you careful to accept, defend, and honor your husband?

12. Proverbs 21:9, 19

Your husband should have confidence that your relationship with him is second only to your relationship with the Lord Himself. Does your husband sense that he is your best friend and number one priority; taking precedence over your children, in-laws, other friends, employers, and even over your church activities?

13. Complete the following quiz to evaluate the quality of "phileo" in your marriage. Rate yourself on the following statements:

Statement Regarding the Quality of Phileo Love in Your Marriage	Weak..........Strong				
	1	2	3	4	5
I never repeat to anyone else the things my husband shares with me privately. (Even in prayer groups.)					
I give my husband my total enthusiastic attention and listen with interest while he becomes more comfortable in expressing himself. (Remember, this is hard for many husbands.)					
I do not interrupt or jump to conclusions about what he is saying or is going to say.					
Even when I disagree with what my husband is saying, I acknowledge that I comprehend, and I repeat his thoughts and feelings back to him so that he is sure I am hearing him. (I try not to let any disagreement sound like personal rejection.)					
When sharing my thoughts, I try successfully not to make my husband feel as if I am heaping blame on him.					
I am available to my husband. Even when it is inconvenient for me, I make a point of sitting down and spending time with him when he is home. I never make him feel like an intruder in my schedule.					
When the children are demanding my attention at the same time that my husband is speaking with me, I am able to focus on my husband.					
I am willing to leave the children with reliable help and get away alone with my husband.					

Note any areas in which you can improve:

Remember that no two people will ever have mastered every facet of but every couple can work to improve their "phileo". "Phileo" is a lifelong process requiring great sensitivity.

Sensitivity means to be aware of your partner as a whole person:

> a) *To recognize your husband's uniqueness,*
> b) *and to discern what will best meet your mate's needs.*

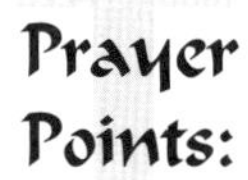

Prayer Points:

Men are different from women. The obvious nature of this statement obscures its profound truth. Learning to "phileo" our husbands requires developing friendship with him through understanding and accepting those differences.

It has been said that when a woman marries she hopes that her husband WILL change, but when a man marries he hopes that his wife WON'T change.

In order to truly learn to love our husbands, we must love them as God has made them. Love covers a multitude of sins (I Peter 4:8).

14. Read I Corinthians 13:7 from "The Living New Testament." Though this speaks of an "agapao" love, it reflects the heart of the Lord as He sees our marriages.

"If you love someone you will be loyal to him no matter what the cost. You will always believe in him, always expect the best of him, and always stand your ground in defending him."
I Corinthians 13:7

If you love your husband this way, will you try to change him?

What Scriptures can you cite that instruct wives to change their husbands?

Is there any area in your husband's life that you have trouble accepting and defending?

What do you think that God wants you to do about it?

Remember, marriage is a covenant relationship (Malachi 2:14). It is an unconditional commitment to an imperfect person. Commitment means a willingness to sometimes be unhappy. We may find that there are times and circumstances that make it more difficult to "phileo" our husbands. Yet, what does Scripture say about being a true friend?

15. Proverbs 17:17

But, what if our mate has some true faults? Aren't we supposed to try to change him under those conditions? Everybody sins (Romans 3:10). Yes, even Christians sin (Romans 7:15-25).

God has established authorities over men that can intervene when civil law is disobeyed. Scripture speaks of these authorities as being established by God Himself (Romans 13:1). Knowing the fallen nature of men and women, the Lord has dealt with this in His Word. There are sadly rare occasions when civil authority must intervene as a last resort.

Most "faults" that are encountered in the home are not civil issues, but are domestic issues. A godly wife's response to a husband's faults is clearly shown in Scripture. We are to speak the truth with a loving attitude (Ephesians 4:15) while demonstrating respectful and pure behavior toward our husbands (I Peter 3:2).

We are called to nurture a forgiving attitude toward our husbands, trusting God to deal with our husbands in His time and in His way. God gives strength to those who wait on Him (Isaiah 40:29-31). We are not called upon to change our husbands. Only God can do that. We are, however, responsible for our own attitudes and responses.

Seeing sin in our husband's life should be our signal to begin to examine our own actions and attitudes.

16. Matthew 7:1-5

The irritating "splinters" that we see in our mate's life often reveal a deeper and larger "log" embedded in our own hearts. Here are some examples:

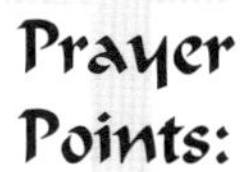

Prayer Points:

- **"splinter"** If a husband's sloppiness is demonstrated by his not picking up his dirty clothes, a wife may resent his apparent laziness.

  "log" Yet, if a wife resents picking up her husband's clothes this reveals that she, too, has a lazy attitude.

- **"splinter"** A wife may be unhappy because she thinks that her husband needs to make more money.

  "log" Yet, the husband may sense that his wife is materialistic and should learn to live within a tighter budget.

- **"splinter"** A wife may feel that her husband does not discipline the children properly.

  "log" Yet, the husband may sense that his wife undermines his authority in the home by going behind his back or overruling his decisions.

- **"splinter"** A wife may feel that her husband is insensitive and selfish because he doesn't seem to notice or appreciate what she does for him.

  "log" The husband may view his wife as being selfish because she doesn't notice or appreciate him. He may sense that her actions are motivated solely by her desire to receive personal praise.

a) What are some of your mate's "splinters?"

b) What would your husband say are some of your "logs?"

Nurturing a "phileo" relationship with our husband is often the catalyst that stirs him to become the man that God has called him to be. We must be trained to love and accept our husband as God created him; the result will be that we become the woman that God has called us to be.

17. In order to more fully demonstrate "phileo" love toward your husband, what specific changes do you need to make in your life?

When will you begin to make those changes?

Commit your decisions to the Lord, asking Him to give you the grace that He has promised in order to enable you to "abound in every good work" (II Corinthians 9:8).

"This is my lover, this is my friend..."
Song of Solomon 5:16

SUMMARY:

Define "phileo" in your own terms. You could use a synonym, a motto, a poem or a prayer, or even make a drawing to show your understanding of this quality.

Prayer Points:

DISCUSSION:

In past generations, did we see more opportunity for older women to train younger women? What has changed? What can we do about it?

APPLICATION:

Your sister in another state had a new baby six months ago. She phones you in tears saying that her husband is insisting that she go away with him for the weekend. She feels that your brother-in-law needs to grow up and realize that the children need her now more than he does. What advice do you give her?

CHAPTER FOUR

BE "ONE FLESH" WITH YOUR HUSBAND

Joyfully embracing sexual intimacy with my husband as being a divine gift from God.

"For this reason a man shall leave his father and his mother, and be joined to his wife; and they shall become one flesh."
Genesis 2:24

"This is my lover, this is my friend..."
Song of Solomon 5:16 (NIV)

For this reason a man shall leave his father and his mother, and be joined to his wife; and they shall become one flesh.
Genesis 2:24

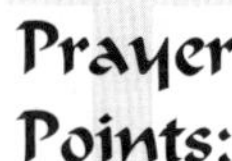

Prayer Points:

Why do people get married? Though certain qualities may attract us to various individuals, why do we enter into the marriage covenant with that one unique person?

We may sense a need for companionship, and friendship is certainly one desired component of marriage. However, it is possible to have a good friend of the opposite sex without entering into the marriage covenant.

Marriage is the only relationship designed by God to satisfy the desire to share physical intimacy by becoming "one flesh."

The very word, "sex," evokes a vast array of thoughts and emotions from every individual. Much of our response stems from our own background, personal experience, and cultural upbringing. Before we begin our study, in the spaces below, write three words that describe your reaction when you hear the word "sex."

a)

b)

c)

Let's begin by going back to the beginning.

1. Genesis 1:27, 28

   In what image were male and female created? (The term "man" as used in this passage is generic.)

   After God blessed them, what was His first command to the male and female?

   What does this tell you about sexuality?

Did God ordain the sexual relationship before, or after, sin entered the world? (See Genesis 3)

Prayer Points:

2. Genesis 1:31

By implication, what was God's evaluation of His design for the sexual relationship between male and female?

In chapter two of Genesis we find a more detailed account of the creation of man and woman. After God fashioned a woman using Adam's rib, He then brought her to the man. It is noteworthy that Adam was given the privilege of determining what a female would be called (2:23). He did not simply call her "man #2," rather, in naming her "woman," he recognized that she was similar to, but very different from himself.

3. Genesis 2:23-25

What does this passage tell you about dealing with in-laws in the marriage relationship?

What was God's intention for the man and his wife?

How did the man and woman react to their nakedness?

4. I Corinthians 6:16-18

In light of this passage, what does it mean to become "one flesh?"

5. Matthew 19:4-6

What role does God play in making a couple "one flesh?"

We are missing much of the meaning behind the sexual relationship if we believe that physical intimacy was intended to be limited to procreation. The concept of becoming "one flesh" does not directly refer to having children. While children are always a gift from God (Psalm 127:3), the sexual relationship between a husband and a wife was designed by God for many reasons.

6. Genesis 24:67

What is one benefit of sex in marriage?

Have you found this to be true in your relationship with your husband?

The sexual relationship in marriage is a gift from God, intended for pleasure. Yet, Satan has taken God's gift of physical intimacy and perverted it. Because of sin, God's gifts are often misrepresented and abused. Sadly, many Christian wives misunderstand this blessing that God designed for them to enjoy. Many women erroneously view sex as being sinful, dirty, or unspiritual.

It is important to note that in the Old Testament, the same Hebrew word is used to describe the way that we love God (Deuteronomy 6:5), the way that we love our neighbor (Leviticus 19:18), and the way that we physically love our spouse (Song of Solomon 7:6). The Lord sees the physical union of a married couple as being of divine decree. It is holy and "very good."

Once Christian wives realize that sensual love is a gift from God, we should experience freedom to enjoy His blessings in this area of our lives. In Scripture, the act of physical consummation is often referred to in terms of drinking from your own well (Proverbs 5:15). In the Song of Solomon, we read a detailed account of the love relationship between a new bride and her husband.

7. Song of Solomon 4:16

How would you describe the new bride's attitude regarding sex?

8. Song of Solomon 5:1b

In this passage we read God's instructions to the couple on their wedding night. What does this tell you about how God views sexual intimacy?

Prayer Points:

Later, the new bride says that, "my heart began to pound for him" (5:4 NIV), and she describes herself as being "faint with love" (5:8 NIV). She is enjoying her physical relationship with her husband.

9. Song of Solomon 5:10-16

What attitude does the new bride have regarding her husband's nakedness?

10. Song of Solomon 7:1-10

As the husband describes his wife's naked body, and he expresses his desire for physical intimacy with her, how does she respond?

How do you respond to your husband under similar situations?

Many women fail to understand that while a woman is responsive to her husband's touch and words (I Corinthians 7:1), a man is stimulated visually (Judges 14:3, 7; II Samuel 11:2). Modesty in apparel is mandated by God (I Timothy 2:9). Godly women are to wear clothing that will not "defraud" men (1 Thessalonians 4:6). To defraud another literally means "to arouse desires in another which cannot be righteously satisfied." Make it your sincere goal to dress in such a way

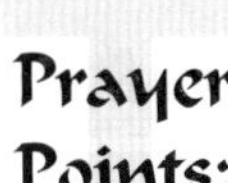

Prayer Points:

that your appearance will not visually lead a man into lust. Yet, the marriage relationship is unique to every relationship on earth. A husband and wife can righteously satisfy each other's desires and bring glory to the Lord. Within the purity of marriage we should be "naked and not ashamed."

Since your husband is physically stimulated by what he sees, what specific steps might you take to enhance this area of your love-life? Begin by considering the following questions:

- Do I wear what my husband likes to see me wear, or do I only wear what pleases me?
- When my husband leaves home each morning, what is generally his last image of me?
- When my husband returns home in the evening, do I make an attempt to look my best for his arrival?
- Do I fix my hair in the style that my husband prefers?
- When was the last time that I wore new lingerie?
- Have I ever asked my husband what he likes for me to wear to bed?
- Do I take care of myself physically in order to look as attractive as possible to my husband?

In the space below, write any changes that you might make in order to enhance your husband's "vision."

Optional: Look up the word "knew" as used in Genesis 4:1, 17, 25 and Matthew 1:24, 25. What insights regarding sexual intimacy might you glean from these words?

When God instituted the union of a man and a woman, He instructed that the man should "cleave" (KJV) to his wife. The word translated from Genesis, "cleave," literally means "to cling or adhere, to abide fast, to overtake and pursue." In the New Testament when the word "cleave" is used, it means "to stick like glue, cemented, welded together so that they cannot be separated."

Prayer Points:

When "two become one," they are fused together in every area of their lives. God considers being "one flesh" to be of high importance in marriage. What do the following passages teach us about marital sexuality?

11. I Corinthians 7:2-5

Based on this passage, how available does God want you to be in order to meet your husband's sexual needs?

Under what conditions might you forego having sexual relations with your husband? Is this a permanent, long-term agreement? Why or why not?

12. Hebrews 13:4

13. I Corinthians 6:9

14. I Thessalonians 4:3-8

What is God's will for you?

To "defraud" means "to take advantage" of another person. It carries with it the idea of arousing desires in another that cannot be righteously satisfied.

Some women are in the habit of flirting. It is possible for a woman to defraud a man, "leading him on," without physically committing the act of overt adultery. Yet, according to verse 6, what does God say that He will do about one who "defrauds" another?

15. Leviticus 20:10-16

What types of things does God specifically forbid in the expression of our sexuality?

16. Exodus 20:14

There are many women who never commit the physical act of adultery; yet, they find themselves enjoying things such as:

Watching T.V. shows where people discuss the details of their adulterous and perverse activities.

Reading sensual romance novels.

Discussing the seamy details of immorality in the news.

Fantasizing about what their lives would be like if they were married to another man.

Going to movies that overtly romanticize sex outside of marriage.

17. Matthew 5:27-30

In God's eyes, what constitutes "adultery?"

How seriously does the Lord consider this problem to be?
Is there anything that you need to change in this area of your life?

18. II Corinthians 10:5

What does this tell you about your thought life?

19. Ephesians 5:12

What should believing women NOT discuss?

Prayer Points:

Sex, as ordained by God, is a holy and a pleasurable gift. When a man and a woman become "one flesh," they experience one of the most intimate, delightful relationships that a human can know.

Becoming "one" does not mean that one individual dominates the other. When a couple becomes "one," they merge to become more than the sum of their parts. Sex is not a question of dominating another person. Rather, sex is the mutual giving of oneself completely to the one whom you love. It is not a question of possessing another person. Rather, sex is the total giving away of one's self to another.

20. Song of Solomon 2:16a; 6:3; 7:10

Write out what the new bride says in each of the verses below:

2:16a

6:3a

7:10

Do the above verses, taken in sequence, reveal any change in the perspective and attitude of the new bride as she contemplates "being one flesh" with her husband? Explain your answer.

How do your personal feelings about marital sex correlate with what God tells us in His Word? Give your honest responses to the following statements:

Prayer Points:

What I Really Think About Being "One Flesh" in Marriage	Disagree.........Agree				
	1	2	3	4	5
I think that sex is way overrated in marriage, so I try to avoid physical intimacy with my husband as much as possible.					
Because I realize that my husband is visually stimulated when it comes to our sexual relationship, I am making a sincere effort to look attractive for him.					
I want to be a "one man woman" in my heart, so I am taking steps to make sure that the things I discuss and think about are righteous and pure.					
I believe that God ordained the sexual relationship in marriage solely for the purpose of "being fruitful and multiplying."					
My husband and I openly communicate with each other regarding our sexuality.					
Because God initiated and ordained the sexual relationship, I believe that physical intimacy with my husband is pure, holy, and good.					
My husband knows that I love him, and he understands that it's all right for me to do a little flirting with other men. He knows I'm just having fun.					
Since I know that God designed sex in marriage for my pleasure, I am able to experience wonderful delight in every aspect of physical intimacy with my husband.					

As you examined God's Word regarding being "one flesh" with your husband, did you discover anything about your relationship that needs to be changed or improved upon?
If so, ask the Lord to give you His mind on the issue, and then begin to take the necessary steps that will enable you and your husband to enjoy all that God designed for you to experience!

"This is my lover, this is my friend..."
Song of Solomon 5:16 NIV

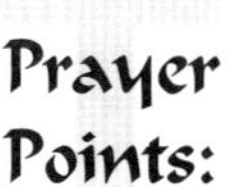

Prayer Points:

SUMMARY:

Define being "one flesh" in your own terms. You could use a synonym, a motto, a poem or a prayer, or even make a drawing to show your understanding of this phrase.

DISCUSSION:

Since the "sexual revolution" of the 1960s, there has been an undeniable increase in promiscuity and immorality in society. Burgeoning numbers of couples live together outside of marriage. What specific things can Christian women do to encourage others to remain sexually pure?

APPLICATION:

One of your Christian friends shares that she enjoys watching "soap operas" every afternoon on T.V. because the men on the shows are so romantic and passionate. She tells you that she sees nothing wrong with vicariously imagining herself in a relationship with one of these male stars. What do you say to your friend?

CHAPTER FIVE

BE A SUITABLE HELPER

Assisting my husband in becoming all that God uniquely designed him to be.

"Then the LORD God said, 'It is not good for the man to be alone; I will make him a helper suitable for him.'"
Genesis 2:18

"Then the LORD God said, 'It is not good for the man to be alone; I will make him a helper suitable for him.'" Genesis 2:18

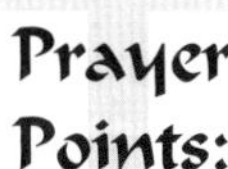

Prayer Points:

The source of many women's problems today is discontent with the purposes and activities for which God created us.

In chapter two of the Genesis Creation account, we discover the marital "Gap Theory." We see that Adam was incomplete and was missing something. He had "gaps." The Creator filled those gaps in Adam's life by creating Eve.

Woman was made from man's rib bone;
not from his foot to be trodden upon,
not from his head to rule over man,
but from near his heart to be loved,
and from under his arm
to be protected and cherished.

(Matthew Henry, late 1600's)

It has been said that after man's rib was taken out to make a woman, man could literally never be complete without her. Man's counterpart needed to be someone like himself spiritually and intellectually; someone who could understand him, sympathize with him, and be the complement of him. He needed someone to fill his gaps. Scripture tells us that it is God's will for certain individuals not to marry (I Corinthians 7:7, 8). Yet, most men do sense an incompleteness that a wife fulfills.

Eve's "gaps" were also filled in the process as she fulfilled the role for which God had created her. What do you learn about a woman's role in marriage from the following texts?

1. Genesis 2:18-25 and I Corinthians 11:8, 9.

   Why did God create woman?

   a)

   b)

c)

d)

Prayer Points:

2. Song of Solomon 2:3-6

3. Ecclesiastes 4:9-12, 9:9

4. Psalm 34:3

The Old English word from Genesis 2:18, translated "helpmeet" (KJV), is actually a combination of two Hebrew words meaning "helper" plus "suitable."

A "helper" is one who assists in order to make it easier for another person to do something.

Webster's New World College Dictionary defines "help" this way;

a) to make things easier or better for (a person); aid; assist; specif.,

1) To give (one in need or trouble) something necessary, as relief, succor, money, etc (to help the poor)
2) To do part of the work of; ease or share the labor of (to help someone lift a load)
3) To aid in getting (up, down, in, etc., or to, into out of, etc) (help her into the house).

b) To make it easier for (something) to exist, happen, develop, improve.

"Suitable" is defined this way;

a) *That which suits a given purpose, occasion, condition, propriety, etc; fitting; appropriate.*

5. As you read the Scripture passages related to why women were created, and as you read the definitions of "suitable helper," what was your reaction? (Be honest)

The very word "helper" rankles many women because we live in a society that tells us we should "look out for number one." Of course, number one is yourself! Our culture is engrossed with personal rights.

We have been erroneously programmed to think of a helper as one occupying a lesser position. We think of a helper as an inferior who is perhaps not as bright, not as well educated, and certainly not very highly motivated.

What do the following verses reveal about being a helper?

6. Psalm 40:17

7. Hebrews 13:6

8. John 14:16, 17

We can see that being a helper means that we are in good company! It is an honor to have opportunity in life to reflect how we are made in the image of God.

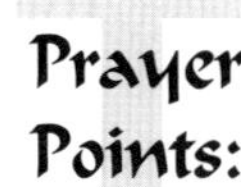

Prayer Points:

Being a helper is not a sign of inferiority; rather, it speaks of our desire to meet the needs of those whom we love.

When we accept God's design for us to be suitable helpers for our husbands, our attitudes become radically changed. Rather than competing with our husbands for the position of "boss," we are free to join with them in pulling toward the same goals.

Being a helper is not a sign of weakness. It is not taking the easy way out. On the contrary, serving others is hard work.

Donning the mantle of "helpmeet," we eagerly leap into action. Yet, very quickly the question arises, "What am I supposed to be helping my husband to do?"

Exactly HOW are we to help our husbands?

9. Genesis 1:26; I Corinthians 11:7

   How was man created?

Adam, though a unique individual, is a prototype of all men. God's commands to him apply to all men, and when Adam broke God's commands all men since have suffered the consequences (Romans 5:12). As we look at the events and purposes behind God's creation of Adam, we can glean much about God's purposes for men universally.

10. Genesis 1:26-2:15. We see that God created man with specific drives and responsibilities. The Lord gave him five specific instructions. While some of these directives were also given to women, our intent here is to discern how to better understand and help our husbands.

    a) EXERCISE DOMINION OVER THE EARTH - Genesis 1:28
    This basic drive is seen in a man's instinct to work, provide for the family, and to dominate and rule with authority.

Optional: Over what specific things was Adam given dominion?

What examples of man's dominion are seen in the following examples?

Joshua 24:15

Genesis 18:19

Psalm 8:6-8

I Timothy 2:12, 13

I Timothy 5:8

I) Give one example of how your husband demonstrates "exercising dominion over the earth." How does he show authority and rulership in your marriage, in the home, on the job, through his hobbies, etc.?

II) Who would you say is the "leader" in your home?

Who would your husband say is the "leader?"

Who would your children say is the "leader?"

b) SUBDUE THE EARTH - Genesis 1:26-30
This drive deals with bringing the forces of nature under control. Incorporated here is man's instinct to work in order to provide food and shelter for the family. Using the principles

of natural and physical science, this drive is the basis of all technological progress.

I) Give one example of how your husband demonstrates "subduing the earth." How does he work to bring the elements of nature under control at home, on the job, through his hobbies, etc.?

Prayer Points:

c) BE FRUITFUL AND MULTIPLY - Genesis 1:28
The sexual drive is a part of the total Christian life.

I) Have you recognized this trait in your husband as being a drive given by God Himself?

II) What have you done recently to keep this area of your marriage fresh?

Children are a gift from God (Psalm 127:3), and yet the Lord has ordained that some women will not bear children. God's plans are perfect, and He uses the lives of childless couples to accomplish special purposes (Acts 18:2, 3, 26: Romans 16:3, 4; 1 Corinthians 16:9).

d) DRESS (tend, cultivate) THE GARDEN - Genesis 2:15
This drive is reflected in the man's drive to delineate his own territory and to care for it.

I) Give one example of how your husband demonstrates "tending his garden." In what ways do you see him uniquely "staking out" and caring for his territory in your marriage, at home, on the job, through his hobbies, etc.?

Prayer Points:

II) Does your husband sense that the home is "his" or is it "yours?" Be alert that if you notice your husband spending most of his time in only one area. (example: garage, yard, or private study), you may have inadvertently taken over all of the areas of your home,

e) KEEP (guard) THE GARDEN - Genesis 2:15
Man possesses an innate desire to exhibit strength in protecting that for which he is responsible. He is driven to protect physically, mentally, emotionally and spiritually.

I) Give one example of how your husband demonstrates "guarding his garden." How do you see his protective nature exhibited in your marriage, in your home, on the job, through his hobbies, etc.?

Were the above commands for men given to Adam before or after he sinned?

What did God call His creation before man sinned? (Genesis 1:31)

What can you conclude about God's opinion of man's basic drives as mentioned above?

Many stresses in the marital relationship come from a lack of acceptance of God's design for our partner. When a wife fails to understand the basic God-given role of her husband, she becomes critical and tries to change him.

A wife can mistakenly consider something to be a fault in her husband that is actually a built-in male characteristic. For example, his compulsion to work extra hours on the job may be misinterpreted by a wife that the husband does not want to spend time at home. In actuality, the husband may be fulfilling his drive to "subdue the earth."

11. Can you think of any areas of conflict in your marriage where you may be misunderstanding your husband's God-given drives?

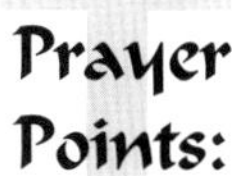

Prayer Points:

In order to be well-suited (tailor-made) for our husband, we are wise to become a student of him. We need to ask the Lord to give us wisdom and understanding in order for us to discern what is important to him, and "what makes him tick" (II Timothy 2:7, James 1:5).

12. Colossians 2:2, 3

What does Paul pray will precede wisdom?

Who is the Source of true wisdom?

A wise wife will discern areas where she can come alongside to assist or encourage her husband as he pushes toward fulfilling the goals that God has established for his life. In doing so, wives do not lose their own purpose in life; rather, it is in this very area that they find their greatest fulfillment. Each man responds to the drives in his life differently as he uses his unique talents, gifts, and strengths.

In addition to these five basic drives, God has given men many specific commands and directives. As our husband's "suitable helper," we are uniquely qualified to help him fulfill what God created him to be, rather than to try to change or remold him. The wise wife discerns specific ways in which she can come alongside her husband to uniquely assist and encourage him.

Make a habit of asking your husband what his goals are for the week. Ask what you can do to help him, or if there is anything that you could change that would make his life easier.

13. Complete the tables on the following pages. The Bible reference with God's instruction to man are provided in the left two columns. Column three provides additional related Bible references that may help to illuminate your understanding of this command as it applies to your marriage. Add any additional Scripture that you may find to this list. Column four, entitled "How I Can Help My Husband," lists several applications for wives. Add any specific ways YOU can help YOUR husband to this list.

Bible Reference	God's Instruction for Man	Related Bible Reference(s)	How I Can I Help My Husband
Genesis 1:28	Be fruitful, multiply, fill the earth	1 Corinthians 7:2-51 Thessalonians 4:3-8 Proverbs 5:15-19 Psalm 127:3-5 Psalm 113:9 Song of Solomon 5:1	Desire Children / be a joyful mother Be available physically Abstain from immorality
Genesis 1:28	Subdue the earth	Genesis 6, 7 Ecclesiastes 2:4-6 Proverbs 31:16	Appreciate his interest in natural science Buy him a shovel, woodworking tools, etc. Thank him for maintaining the cars Joyfully accompany him on camping trips
Genesis 1:28	Rule over the living creatures	I Samuel 17:34-36 Ecclesiastes 2:3-6 Proverbs 31:16	Praise him for training the dog Buy him a fishing pole Always follow his lead; support his decisions Thank him for disciplining the children
Genesis 1:29	Eat plants (later also meat, Genesis 9:2)	Acts 10:12-15 Proverbs 31:14, 15 Ecclesiastes 2:25l Corinthians 10:25, 31	Grocery shop Cook healthy foods that he likes Help him plant a vegetable garden Clip coupons

Bible Reference	God's Instruction for Man	Related Bible Reference(s)	How I Can Help My Husband
Genesis 2:15	Tend the Garden	Titus 2:3-51 Timothy 5:14 Proverbs 24:27 Proverbs 27:18	Maintain home; decorate, clean
Genesis 2:15	Keep the Garden	Proverbs 22:29 Proverbs 24:3-5l Timothy 5:8	Thank him for installing alarm system Cooperate with his home-safety campaigns Be gentle; don't be independent or tough Thank him for his physical protection Appreciate his career and work-ethic
Genesis 2:17-18	Obey God	Proverbs 31:11-13; 28-30 Colossians 3:23, 24 Acts 16:30, 31 Joshua 24:15	Express your commitment to obey God Praise acts of obedience on his part Allow him to grow spiritually at his own pace Pray for him
Genesis 2:19	Name the creatures	I Kings 5:29-34	Point out and appreciate the variety in God's creation

Prayer Points:

Obedience to God's design in marriage will often yield unexpected joy and blessing in your life. Be careful that your motive in being a helper to your husband is not self-serving. Your goal should never be to manipulate or change your husband. Our motive as wives should always be a sincere desire to please our Lord (II Corinthians 5:9). Even when we do not feel like helping our husbands, we help them because God wants us to; it brings Him glory.

14. Philippians 2:13, 14

    As God is at work in you, what two things does He do in your life?

    Why does God work in your life?

    As we obediently do God's will, what should we be careful to avoid?

In considering how to help your husband, has the Holy Spirit prompted you in any specific area where you need to more readily serve your husband? If so, note that area in the space below.

Purpose in your heart, that by God's grace, you will begin today to help your husband in those areas listed above.

Remember, there is no other woman on the face of the planet who is better suited to meet your husband's needs than you are. If you do not help your husband, he will not receive the help that God intended for him to experience in his life. Thank the Lord for your husband. Ask God to give you the opportunity to begin helping him in new ways; then DO IT!

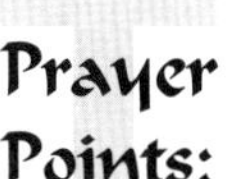

Prayer Points:

SUMMARY:

Define "suitable helper" in your own terms. You could use a synonym, a motto, a poem or a prayer, or even make a drawing to show your understanding of this phrase.

DISCUSSION:

Why do you think that American women today react so strongly against the concept of having been created to be a "helper" for their husbands?

Is this attitude new with this generation?

APPLICATION:

A Christian woman tells you that the Old Testament roles for women and men became passe with the advent of Christ. She cites Galatians 3:28 which states;

**"There is neither male nor female;
for you are all one in Christ Jesus."**

How do you respond?

CHAPTER SIX

BE SUBJECT TO YOUR OWN HUSBAND
-Attitudes-

Willingly choosing to yield humble and intelligent obedience to my husband

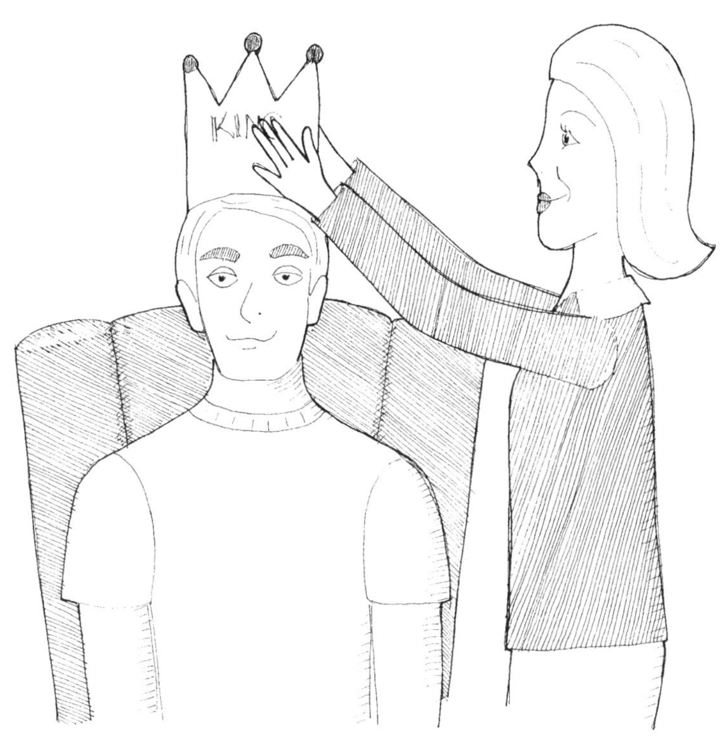

"Wives, be subject to your own husbands, as to the Lord."
Ephesians 5:22

"Wives, be subject to your own husbands, as to the Lord."
Ephesians 5:22

Prayer Points:

The "S" word. Submission. The very mention of the word evokes strong reactions. Lengthy computerized printouts enumerating a hostile plethora of arguments entitled, "Why I will never be submissive," come rolling out of the minds of contemporary women.

As women who desire to walk in God's ways, we must seriously grapple with the issue of wives "submitting to," or "being subject to," their husbands. The first question that must be asked is whether or not God REALLY instructs women to be subject to their husbands.

The answer to that question is an undeniable "yes." The principle of submission is found throughout the entire Bible, along with abundant examples of women who were and were not submissive to their husbands.

While Scripture exhorts all believers to "be subject to one another" (Ephesians 5:21), there is a special emphasis placed on God's desire for women to subject themselves to their own husbands. In every New Testament discussion of marriage the direct instruction for wives to submit to their husbands is repeated.

What are the arguments that women use to support their refusal to seriously consider obeying God's command to be subject to their own husbands?

- ❐ "I think marriage should be 50/50."
- ❐ "I'm equal with my husband, not beneath him."
- ❐ "I refuse to become a doormat. Forget it."
- ❐ "I'm intelligent and perfectly capable of standing on my own two feet."
- ❐ "It was only meant for illiterate women of Bible times."
- ❐ "I'm not about to let any man, even my husband, tell me how to run my life."
- ❐ "I tried it before and felt that it wasn't very joyful. God wants me to be happy, so I've decided not to be submissive."
- ❐ "The only person I have to be submissive to is God."
- ❐ "If I didn't run this family it would fall apart."

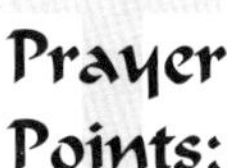

Prayer Points:

Put a checkmark beside any of the above arguments which you yourself have thought, or which you have encountered from others.

Much of the hostility and resistance related to being submissive reflects confusion about what submission actually means.

Webster's New Collegiate Dictionary defines "submission" as:

1) *the act of submitting, yielding; or surrendering*
2) *the quality or condition of being submissive; resignation obedience; meekness*
3) *the act of submitting something to another for decision, consideration, etc.*
4) *In Law an agreement whereby parties to a dispute submit the matter to arbitration and agree to be bound by the decision*

When God speaks of a wife being "subject to," or "submissive" to, her husband, the Greek word, "hupotasso," is used. "Hupotasso" is comprised of two words;

1) "hupo," meaning "to place under" and
2) "tasso," meaning "to place, set, appoint, arrange, order."

It literally means "to place under in an orderly fashion." "Hupotasso" is primarily a military term meaning "to rank under." It is a voluntary action; not one of enforced servitude. In other words, a wife is to make the choice to place herself, or rank herself, underneath her husband.

Submission has been defined as "yielding humble and intelligent obedience to an ordained power or authority." It is both an attitude and an action.

In this chapter we will examine the wife's attitude of submission, and in the next chapter we will look at how the proper attitude manifests itself in actions. Many questions may be raised that are not dealt with in this chapter. We will look more closely at the "what ifs" and "buts" in Chapter 7 as we go into more detail. Please don't get discouraged; hang in there!

Let's begin by examining our attitude regarding submission.

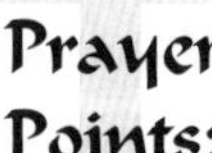

Prayer Points:

Optional: Using your concordance and Bible dictionary, look up all of the various relationships described by the term "hupotasso" in Scripture. Does this give you any insight into the way that you are to be subject to your husband?

A woman's "natural" reaction to the concept of submission is one of resistance (I Corinthians 2:14), but God has not called Christian women to live a "natural" life. The Lord wants us to live in a "supernatural" way as we are filled with His Spirit (Galatians 5:22-25).

Why do believing wives find it difficult to maintain an attitude of submission toward their husbands?

Many women question whether or not the Bible really instructs women to "be subject" to their husbands. Has God ordained a structure of authority in marriage? Read the following verses to determine the husband's role and the wife's position in marriage.

1. Ephesians 5:22-24; Colossians 3:18, Titus 2:5

Note that God only instructs wives to be subject to their own husbands, not to all men in general.

2. Romans 13:1, 2

   What does this passage tell you about authority?

   What does this passage tell you about resisting authority?

   How might this apply to your relationship with your husband?

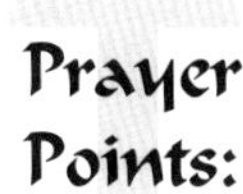

Prayer Points:

Some women feel that to be submissive to their husbands would be a sign of inequality. After all, Scripture tells us that in Christ "there is neither Jew nor Greek, slave nor free, male nor female, for you are all one in Christ" (Galatians 3:27, 28).

Doesn't that mean that we are all equal in the Lord? Absolutely yes! We are spiritually equal with our husbands. Yet, we hold different positions in the marriage relationship.

3. I Peter 3:7

How does this passage indicate that there is a difference between husbands and wives?

How does this passage indicate that there is equality between husbands and wives?

To be subject to your husband does not mean that you are not equal to your husband. Submission is a voluntary action that in no way signifies inferiority.

Some suggest that being subject to their husbands is degrading, and is not an honorable position to be held. What does God teach us about this?

4. I Corinthians 15:28

Who is being submissive to Whom in this verse?

Would you refer to this as being "degrading?"

Others may argue that a wife should not be submissive to her husband if he is not as spiritually minded as she is. Should a wife who has more godly wisdom than her husband take over the headship of her marriage? What do the following verses indicate regarding spiritually mature wives who are married to not-so-spiritual husbands?

5. I Peter 3:1, 2

6. I Corinthians 7:13-16

Godly wives are called to be subject to their husbands even if their husbands are not spiritually minded. A wife's attitude of submission may be the catalyst that the Lord uses to bring her husband to a saving knowledge of Christ.

The greatest hindrance to developing an attitude of submission is our own pride. Pride is our enemy. Pride keeps us from denying ourselves. Yet, what does the Lord tell us about self-denial?

7. Luke 9:23

Self-denial and submission are an attitude and a choice.

8. Colossians 3:22-24

Christ is the eternal example of humility and submission.

9. Philippians 2:5-11

According to this passage, in what way are we to be like Christ?

What was Christ's "position" from the beginning?

Because of Christ's "position," what "rights" could He have legally claimed?

How many of those "rights" did He claim?

Who "humbled" Him?

How far did Christ go with His attitude of submission?

Prayer Points:

Do you think that this was difficult for Christ?
(See Hebrews 5:7)

How did the Father honor Christ's submissive obedience?

Who receives the glory from Christ's Self-humbling?

Do you think that what Christ gained as a result of His submission was worth it?

Our pride becomes an obstacle to submission when we begin to believe that something is "our due." We do not have a humble attitude when we cling to certain "rights" that we have claimed.

Consider your marriage. Can you identify any areas where you may have claimed certain "rights?" Put a checkmark beside any statement below that you have heard yourself say in your heart.

- ❑ "All I hear are constant demands; I deserve more 'me' time."
- ❑ "I work hard; I deserve a nicer home and some new clothes."
- ❑ "I do so much for others; my family should show more appreciation."
- ❑ "I don't care if my husband doesn't like it; I'm going to decorate my house the way I want."
- ❑ "It's my money, too; I'm going to spend it however I please."
- ❑ "I'm tired of my husband deciding how we're going to spend our weekends; I'm going to spend my free time how I choose."
- ❑ "I know more about what's going on in this family than my husband does; I should be the one making the decisions.
- ❑ "I deserve some help; my husband should do more household chores."

- ❑ "I'm at least entitled to a full night's sleep."
- ❑ "I deserve to live near my family and friends; I'm not going to relocate just because he has another job opportunity."
- ❑ "I cook five nights a week; I should be taken out to dinner more often."

Any area where we claim personal "rights" is an area where we are proud. Any area in which we are proud, we are not humble. Any area in which we are not humble, we are not submissive. Any area in which we are not subject to our husband is disobedience.

Pride in marriage can be traced back to the Garden of Eden. The very nature of Satan is pride and rebellion (Isaiah 14:13, 14). Our flesh wants to assert itself, not to deny itself. Just as Satan spoke to Eve, he continues to whisper in our ears, "Did God really say......?" (Genesis 3:3). He challenges us to disregard God's instructions and to do whatever we want; whatever looks good and desirable to us (3:5, 6). But the fruit of sin is bitter.

After Eve sinned, what changed regarding her relationship with her husband?

10. Genesis 3:16

What would the woman "desire?"

The word for "desire" here is only found three times in Scripture. The same term is used in Genesis 4:7 where sin is pictured as a crouching animal ready to pounce on Cain in order to gain mastery over him. In the same way, the woman is cursed with the desire to gain mastery over her husband; yet, her husband will rule over her.

When a wife submits herself to her husband's ordained headship in marriage, she denies herself and gives up her desire to be the boss. It is a continual struggle, however, because pride continues to demand its way. Humility is the opposite of pride, and humility is at the core of a submissive attitude. In order to become subject to another, our pride must be slain.

11. James 4:6

Why is it important that we not be proud?

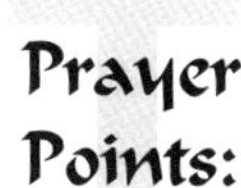

Prayer Points:

What does the Lord give humble people?

Do you want the Lord to give you more of this in your own life? If so, what must you do?

Denying yourself is painful. Christ refers to it in conjunction with taking up your cross (Mark 8:34). Just as Christ denied Himself and was obedient to the point of death on a cross (Philippians 2:8), we are called to die daily (I Corinthians 15:31). Paul tells us that "those who belong to Christ Jesus have crucified the sinful nature with its passions and desires" (Galatians 5:24).

Just as it takes the assistance of another to physically crucify a person, the Lord often uses other individuals to help "nail us down" as we die daily. We must cooperate with that one whom the Lord may use in our lives to help make us more like Jesus. Sometimes, that person is our husband. (In the following chapter we will address the difficult questions regarding how a submissive attitude should affect our specific responses and actions as wives.)

As we cooperate with the Lord and humble ourselves, He gives us His strength to obey. Del Fehsenfeld suggests that a practical definition of "grace" would be "the dynamic quality of God in me that gives me the desire and the power to live in harmony with God and His Word."

Many Christian women will concede that it is good to be subject to their husbands up to a certain point. But, don't you have to draw the line somewhere? How much submission is enough?

Again, consider the example of Christ. How far was He willing to go in order to completely obey the Father? Christ went all the way in being subject to the Father's will. As a result, He is eternally exalted and brings eternal glory to the Father (Philippians 2:9-11).

- The question is not, ***"how far do I have to go in being subject to my husband?"***
- The real question is, ***"how much do I want to glorify God and experience His blessing in my life?"***

- The question is not, ***"how much more can I take?"***
- The real question is, ***"how much more can I give?"***

The pathway to blessing and glory always passes through the doorway of humility.

12. Ephesians 5:22-24

What analogy is used to represent the way in which a wife is to submit to her husband?

Do you have any reservations about Christ being the head of the church?

How much should you be subject to Christ?

What does this tell you about being subject to your own husband?

According to this passage, in what areas should a wife voluntarily be subject to her husband?

God commands our husbands to care for us in the same way that Christ cared for the church. Christ gave everything for us. Our husbands are called upon by God to give everything for their wives. Yet, even if your husband is not obedient to Scripture, God calls you to obey.

While human logic tells us that being submissive will result in our becoming oppressed and downtrodden, Scripture says just the opposite. The Lord tells us that godly submission is a woman's glory.

13. Luke 1:46-48

    How is Mary exalted through submission?

14. Esther 4:16; 9:29-32

    How is Esther exalted through submission?

15. I Peter 5:6

Though wives experience personal blessing when they voluntarily place themselves under the God-ordained authority of their husbands, the most amazing blessing of all is that we are given the great privilege of reflecting Christ. When we are subject to our husbands, all creation looks at our marriage and sees a living picture of Jesus' love relationship with the church.

- Getting practical, is it difficult for you to have a humble attitude and take your proper place in God's chain of command?

- Do you agree with God that your resistance to being subject to your husband is sin? Will you repent of that sin?

- Are there some areas in your marriage where you find it to be especially difficult to subject yourself to your husband? If so, identify those areas in the space below.

Prayer Points:

Remember, it is not hypocritical to submit to our husbands even if we don't feel like it (Romans 12:9, 10). Choosing to subject ourselves to our own husbands is simply an act of obedience to God's will (John 14:15). A hypocrite is someone who does something that she does not feel like doing while saying that she enjoys doing it. It is possible to submit to our husbands with a gentle and quiet spirit (and tongue!).

- ⌘ Thank the Lord for continuing to make you conformed to the image of Christ (Romans 8:29).
- ⌘ Refuse to lean on your own understanding (Proverbs 3:5), and commit your heart and actions to Him (Psalm 37:5).
- ⌘ Ask God to create a clean heart in you, and to give you a right spirit (Psalm 51:10).
- ⌘ Ask the Lord to mercifully enable you to "have this attitude in yourselves which was also in Christ Jesus" (Philippians 2:5-11).

"Let the words of my mouth and the meditation of my heart be acceptable in Your sight, O LORD, my Rock and my Redeemer."
Psalm 19:14

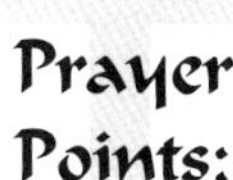

Prayer Points:

SUMMARY:

Define "having an attitude of submission" in your own terms. You could use a synonym, a motto, a poem or a prayer, or even make a drawing to show your understanding of this quality.

DISCUSSION:

In your opinion, what do you see as being the main reason that contemporary women resist the idea of being subject to their husbands?

APPLICATION:

A Christian friend's husband is not saved. Your friend feels that she does not need to be subject to her husband since she knows God's will more than he does. What counsel do you give her?

CHAPTER SEVEN

BE SUBJECT TO YOUR OWN HUSBAND
-Actions-

Willingly choosing to yield humble and intelligent obedience to my husband.

"Wives, be subject to your own husbands, as to the Lord."
Ephesians 5:22

"Wives, be subject to your own husbands, as to the Lord."
Ephesians 5:22

Prayer Points:

Submission has been defined as,

"yielding humble and intelligent obedience to an ordained power or authority."

Biblical submission is the voluntary action of "arranging oneself under one of another rank." In God's ordered "chain of command" in the universe (Romans 13:1, 2), He has determined that in marriage the husband be the head of the wife, and that the wife be subject to her husband (Ephesians 5:22-24; Colossians 3:18; Titus 2:5).

Being subject to your husband involves both an attitude and action. Acts of submission should be preceded by an attitude of submission.

1. Colossians 3:22-24

   Is it possible to "go through the motions" with acts of submission, and yet, not be pleasing to the Lord?

   What pleases the Lord?

   When we serve those in authority over us, who are we really serving?

2. Ephesians 5:33

   What attitude are you to have toward your husband?

   Is there any indication that this attitude must be "earned" by the husband?

What does this tell you about your relationship with your husband?

Prayer Points:

3. I Peter 3:6

In addition to obeying her husband, how did Sarah refer to him?

While a woman's greatest need in marriage is to feel loved and secure, a husband's greatest need is to sense honor and respect from his wife. How does a wife show respect to her husband? Here's how the Amplified Bible expresses Ephesians 5:33b:

"Let the wife see that she respects and reverences her husband– that she notices him, regards him, honors him, prefers him, venerates and esteems him; and that she defers to him, praises him, and loves and admires him exceedingly."

With this in mind, would you say that you respect your husband? A wife who respects her husband will;

- Overtly admire his qualities.
- Never correct him in front of others.
- Learn to depend on him for protection and strength.
- Anticipate and prepare for his returning home each day.
- Never allow his children to be disrespectful toward him.
- Always speak highly of him.
- Always defend his reputation.

Based upon the above criterion, would your husband say that you respect him? A heart attitude of submission must always exude the fragrance of respect.

Once our attitudes are in line with the heart of God, questions inevitably arise regarding the application of Scripture to specific life circumstances in marriage. When the rubber meets the road in our homes, we need to know what submission looks like in a godly wife.

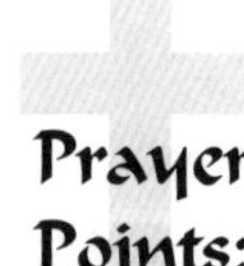

Prayer Points:

QUESTION #1

Does "being subject" mean that a wife should give no input into decisions made in the home?

No. As your husband's "suitable helper," you are designed by the Lord to assist your husband in life. Your husband needs your input. You are a team; but always remember that the team captain is your husband.

Most wives underestimate the influence that they have over their husbands. A wife's godly input can greatly benefit her husband and family for generations to come. Scripture provides accounts of wives whose input impacted their husband's lives for both good and for evil. Take care to always give your husband wise counsel, and once it has been given, be quiet (Proverbs 21:9, 19).

Optional: Look up the following passages that record wives giving input into their husbands lives. What insights can you glean from these examples?

II Kings 4:8-17

Esther 4:15 - 8:3

Daniel 5:5-12

I Kings 21:7-11

Matthew 27:19

QUESTION #2

If a husband does not have good leadership qualities, does God still want the wife to "be subject to him?

Yes. We are to be subject to our husbands even if they are not wise leaders.

4. I Peter 3:1-6

What wife is presented as being the ultimate example of "submission?"

Prayer Points:

The example that Peter chooses to use in his description of a submissive wife is an extreme one. Read the passage below to discern how far this wife went in being subject to her husband.

5. Genesis 12:11-20

What did Abram ask his wife to do?

What was Sarai's response to her husband's sinful request? (Sarah and Sarai are the same person)

6. Genesis 20:1-14

That's right! It happened TWICE! Would you say that Abraham exhibited good leadership skills as a husband?

What did Sarah do this second time?

Scripture presents Sarah as the ultimate model of a wife's submission because the challenges in her marriage were so extreme. Because of her circumstances, Sarah's life presents a case for submission that is absolute.

Sarah's husband was asking her to cooperate in his sin. In spite of Abraham's sin, the Lord protected Sarah from sexual impurity as she trusted in Him (Genesis 20:6). In these passages we see Abraham not only being a fearful leader for his wife; he was taking her in the wrong direction. Yet, Sarah chose to be subject to him. At the end of their story, we see that the Lord blessed both Sarah and Abraham because of their faith (Hebrews 11:8-12).

QUESTION #3

Should a wife be subject to her husband if he is leading her into overt sin?

If a husband tells his wife to participate in a sin against God, the discerning wife will immediately pray about the situation. Wise wives learn to pray regarding their husband's decisions and heart attitudes.

7. Proverbs 21:1

   What can God do with a leader's heart?

After praying and seeking the mind of the Lord, a wise wife will make a respectful appeal to her husband. Information on "How to Make an Appeal" is located at the back of this chapter.

After making her appeal, she should not argue with her husband.

8. I Peter 3:1, 2

   According to this passage, what kind of behavior should the wife demonstrate in order to perhaps win her husband away from disobedience?

A wife's behavior and submission should always be pure. If a husband asks his wife to participate in what is clearly a sin again God, she should respectfully, and prayerfully, refuse.

(A special note regarding physical abuse: In those extreme situations where a wife or child's life may literally be in physical danger, the Lord has established civil authority to protect individuals in the home (I Peter 2:13, 14; Romans 13:1-4). It is not wrong to remove oneself from a life-threatening situation (Acts 9:23, 24, 29, 30).)

QUESTION #4

How can a wife follow a husband who refuses to lead?

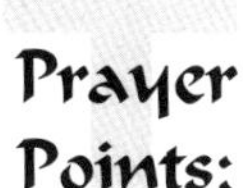

Prayer Points:

Make it your ambition to wait on the Lord to accomplish His purposes in your husband's life. It may be tempting to take over an area of marriage where a husband is not exerting leadership, yet, waiting on the Lord shows that we trust His promises (Psalm 130:5).

Waiting on the Lord also leaves the door open for a husband to eventually begin to assert leadership. If a wife assumes the leadership role, a passive husband may gladly allow it; however, the marriage will fall short of God's best.

If your husband is a "reluctant leader," make it your ambition as a wife to help your husband to lead you.

a) Acknowledge that you need your husband. Recognize your need and guard against developing an independent spirit.

b) Pray for your husband to become your leader. Rather than speaking with your husband about the Lord, speak with the Lord about your husband (I Peter 3:1, 2; I Timothy 2:1, 2; Proverbs 21:1).

c) Wait on God's sovereign timing; trust the Lord (Hebrews 11:11; II Timothy 1:12).

d) Take care to notice those times when your husband does lead; even if his leadership is not what you had envisioned.

e) Assign value to what your husband already does, and communicate your appreciation. Remember, your husband's greatest need is to be honored and respected by you (Ephesians 5:33; I Peter 3:2, 6; I Thessalonians 5:12-14).

f) Express satisfaction and contentment with your husband's provision. Since God has placed your husband over you, your husband's provision is actually God's provision for you. Nurture a thankful heart and develop a quiet spirit (Romans 13:1, 2; I Thessalonians 5:16-18; Philippians 4:11; I Peter 3:4).

g) Allow him to lead, and FOLLOW HIM!

QUESTION #5

Should a wife be subject to a husband whose choices are going to cause difficulty for her and place burdens on the family?

The "fear factor" is a key element in a wife's decision to be subject to her husband.

9. I Peter 3:6

How do women become "Sarah's daughters?"

Why might a wife be fearful of submitting to her husband? When your husband's choices may lead to your personal discomfort, submission becomes frightening.

A submissive wife is totally vulnerable. If her husband fails, she experiences the repercussions. Consider any fears that you might have experienced as you have voluntarily made yourself subject to your husband. Put a checkmark beside any area of fear stated below that you might have experienced.

- ❑ Fear of family suffering financial setbacks, emotional pain, or spiritual loss.
- ❑ Fear of looking foolish in front of others.
- ❑ Fear of enduring your husband's harshness, stubbornness, or pride.
- ❑ Fear of having unfulfilled plans, dreams, and desires.
- ❑ Fear of having to be your husband's "mop-up crew" if he fails.

Rather than fear the consequences of being subject to our husbands, we should instead "be subject to one another in the fear of Christ" (Ephesians 5:21).

Godly wives must relinquish their fear by giving it to the Lord. Wives are to be subject to their husbands "in the same way" that Jesus Christ made Himself submissive (I Peter 3:1).

10. I Peter 2:18-23

According to verse 20, what finds favor with God?

A believer has been called to what purpose?

How do you feel about that "call?"

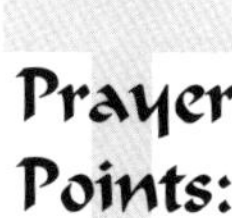

Prayer Points:

How did Christ respond when He was innocently suffering?

What does this tell you about how a wife should respond to suffering when she has been obedient in her actions?

Allow your husband room to fail. God will use that failure in his life to develop godly character in him if you will allow Him to work (Romans 5:3, 4).

11. I John 4:18

How might this apply to the marriage relationship?

When wives surrender themselves to the will of God by being subject to their husbands, they experience surprising benefit.

How does being subject to your husband lead to your protection?

12. I Timothy 2:12-14

13. I Peter 3:7

14. Ephesians 5:26-30

How does a godly wife experience love from her husband?

15. Proverbs 31:28, 29

16. Ephesians 5:24, 25, 33

Prayer Points:

How does an obedient wife experience love from the Lord?

17. John 14:21

God's Word is powerful; it is like fire, and like a hammer which shatters a rock (Jeremiah 23:29). When we obey the Lord in our marriages, God will kindle a fire in our homes, and He will utterly shatter the most resistant obstacles in our lives. We can trust Him. His promises never fail.

- Is it the desire of your heart to relinquish control of your life and yield humble obedience to the Lord in every area of your marriage?

- In light of God's Word, is there any area of your life where you have failed to be subject to your husband as the Lord desires? If so, note those areas in the space below.

- What specific changes do you need to make in the areas mentioned above?

- Are you harboring any fear that may be hindering your ability to be subject to your husband? If so, identify that fear and record it in the space below.

- Spend some time with the Lord in prayer. Confess your fear to Him. Commit yourself to trusting in God; then step out in faith to obey Him.

We know that the woman was created for the man (I Corinthians 11:9). Having a submissive attitude toward the Lord and toward our husband is "doing what is right" (I Peter 3:5, 6). When we follow God's paths we will experience fullness of joy and pleasures forever (Psalm 16:11).

What does a woman gain by submission to her own husband?

- She gains the peace of knowing that she is cooperating with God's plan for her life;
- She experiences the satisfaction of watching her husband become a stronger man each day;
- She delights in knowing that she is pleasing the God of the universe;
- She rests in the assurance that God is in control of every detail of her life;
- She smiles at the knowledge that her life is a picture of the love relationship between Christ and the church;
- She revels in the joy of knowing Christ intimately;
- She overflows in the grace that God gives to those who have humble hearts; and
- She experiences "oneness" with a husband whose love relationship with her grows deeper every day.

When a wife sets her heart on nurturing a God-honoring relationship with her husband, her life becomes a testimony of God's love for all of creation to see. A godly marriage also sets the stage for the Lord to use your home and lives in a special way. Generations of lives will be blessed by your commitment to walking faithfully with the Lord. In the next *Ancient Paths* study, "Walking as Mothers and Homemakers," we will continue to explore our life journey as women of God.

Prayer Points:

"So they are no longer two, but one flesh. What therefore God has joined together, let no man separate."
Matthew 19:6

HOW TO MAKE AN APPEAL

In the first chapter of Daniel we find a handsome Jewish teenager who had been taken captive to Babylon (1:1-3). His intelligence, understanding, discerning knowledge and general ability made Daniel stand out in the crowd (1:4), and he was selected to be trained for the king's personal service (1:5).

As part of his training, Daniel was ordered to eat the king's choice food and to drink wine (1:5). This presented a dilemma for Daniel since it violated his personal spiritual convictions (1:8). It behooves us to note the steps that Daniel took in order to make an appropriate appeal.

1. Discern the heart motive of the one in authority:

Daniel understood that the motive of his superiors was to improve his health and his appearance before the king (1:10).

2. Acknowledge and respect their motives:

Daniel did not argue with the goals of his leaders. He found common ground, and agreed that these goals were worthy (1:12, 13).

3. Ask permission to suggest a creative alternative:

Daniel respectfully requested that he be permitted to attain the king's goals using a method which offered a "win-win" solution for both parties (1:8, 12, 13).

4. Graciously accept the decision of the authority as God's will:

Daniel asked for permission to try the "Jewish diet" for ten days. The results were superior, and Daniel's commitment to maintain his spiritual conviction was authorized (1:11-16).

While we must realize that all authority is established by God (Romans 13:1), and we are to thank God for everything in our lives because it is God's will for us (I Thessalonians 5:16-18), what should be our response if those in authority command us to disobey God's law?

5. Graciously accept the consequence if you must disobey:

Daniel was not forced to disobey God at this time in his life. Yet, he had "made up his mind" that he would not disobey God's law, regardless of the king's decree (1:8).

Later in Daniel's life, we see that he quietly refused to obey the king's order to stop praying to God (6:1-17). He did not argue or defend himself when he was thrown into the lions' den. Daniel trusted God, and he was supernaturally protected (6:16-24).

If we must disobey human authority on biblical grounds, we must be willing to graciously suffer the consequences for the glory of God. The Lord is in control of those in authority over us (Proverbs 21:1), and He is in control of every detail of our lives. We can trust Him!

SUMMARY:

Define "marriage" in your own terms. You could use synonym, a motto, a poem or a prayer, or even make a drawing to show your understanding of this term.

Prayer Points:

DISCUSSION:

Many women today complain that they have become the family leaders by default since their husbands have refused to lead. Is there anything that a wife can do to encourage her husband to become a leader without "ordering him to command?"

APPLICATION:

For married women:
A Christian friend's husband is not saved. He has told her that rather than going to church Sunday mornings that he wants her to stay home with the family. What counsel do you give her?

For single women:
As an unmarried woman, is there anyone to whom you should "submit" or "be subject to?"

Recommended Reading, References and Resources

Chapters 1 and 2:

Learning to Be a Woman, Kenneth G. Smith, InterVarsity Press, 1971
Disciplines of a Beautiful Woman, Anne Ortlund, Word Books, 1978

Chapter 3:

The Christian Family, Larry Christenson, Bethany Fellowship, 1970
Living New Testament, Tyndale House Foundation, Wheaton, IL1967

Chapter 4:

Sexual Happiness in Marriage, Herbert J. Miles Ph.D., Zondervan Publishing House, 1967
Different By Design, John MacArthur, Jr., Victor Books, 1994
Love Life For Every Married Couple, Ed Wheat, M.D., Zondervan Publishing House, 1980
Marriage Without Regrets, Kay Arthur, Precept Ministries of Reach Out, Inc., 1988

Chapter 5:

Design For Christian Marriage, Dwight Small, Fleming H. Revell, 1959

Chapters 6 and 7:

The Feminine Principle, Judith Miles
On The Other Side of the Garden, Virginia Fugate, Alpha and Omega Publications, 1992
Self-Confrontation Manual, (chapter 15), J. C. Broger, Biblical Counseling Foundation, 1991
Strengthening Your Marriage, Wayne Mack, Presbyterian and Reformed Publishing Company, 1977
Me? Obey Him?, Elizabeth Rice Hanford, Sword of the Lord Publishers, 1972

Unless otherwise noted, all Bible quotations used in this study are taken from the NASB version of the Holy Bible

How to Do the *OPTIONAL Word Studies

The ***OPTIONAL*** word studies from each chapter are designed to enhance your understanding of each week's lesson. In order to do these ***OPTIONAL*** studies you will need access to some books that will broaden your ability to study the Bible for yourself.

There are two basic approaches recommended for doing your word studies.

1. The first approach requires two study resource books:

· Strong's Exhaustive Concordance of the Bible; James Strong, S.T.D., LL.D.; MacDonald Publishing Company, McLean, Virginia, 22102.

· Vine's Complete Expository Dictionary of Old and New Testament Words; W. E. Vine, Merrill F. Unger, William White, Jr.; Copyright 1985 by Thomas Nelson Publishers.

An exhaustive concordance is a book containing every word of the text of the Bible, and every occurrence of each word in sequential order. It is important to use a concordance that is compatible with the translation version of Scripture that you are using.

Concordance words are arranged alphabetically by topic. Underneath the highlighted word that you are studying, you will find the abbreviated Bible references, in sequential order, of every place where that word is located in Scripture. Printed to the right of each reference is the text where that word is used in the Bible. To the far right of the printed text you will see a code number.

In the back of your concordance are located two dictionaries; the Old Testament dictionary is in Hebrew, and the New Testament Dictionary is in Greek. Look up the code number in the appropriate dictionary, and you will find the exact word used in the original language, along with the definition of that word.

If you would like more in-depth study of the original meaning of that word, you may use a Vine's Expository Dictionary of Old and New Testament Words. The Expository Dictionary is organized alphabetically in English, and amplifies the abbreviated definition that you will find in the back of your concordance. The code numbers located in Vine's are the same as Strong's Concordance numbers.

2. *The second approach requires three study resource books:*

- The Complete Word Study New Testament; Spiros Zodhiates, Th.D.; Copyright 1991 by AMG International, Inc. Publishers, Chattanooga, TN, 37422

If you would like more in-depth study of the original meaning of that word, you may use:

- The Complete Word Study Old Testament; Spiros Zodhiates, Th.D.; Copyright 1994 by AMG International, Inc. D/B/A AMG Publishers, Chattanooga, TN, 37422

- The Complete Word Study Dictionary New Testament; Spiros Zodhiates, Th.D.; Copyright 1992 by AMG International, Inc. Publishers, Chattanooga, TN, 37422

The Complete Word Study New and Old Testaments contain the entire Biblical texts in the King James Version. As you read the text, you will find a code number above each word. The Word Study Testaments use a numbering system that is compatible with both Vine's Expository Dictionary and Strong's Exhaustive Concordance. These numbers are all interchangeable. Look up that number in the dictionary located in the back of your Word Study Testament. There you will find the precise meaning of the word as used in the original language.

If you want further elaboration of the meaning of a New Testament word, you can use The Complete Word Study Dictionary New Testament. At this time, a Word Study Dictionary of the Old Testament has not yet been published. This New Testament dictionary is organized numerically, rather than topically, in English. Look up your code number in the dictionary to find a more in-depth definition of the word that you are studying.

Glossary

- Called – designated, invited, set apart by an action of God to some spiritual sphere and manner of being
- Confession – to agree with God by openly admitting personal guilt regarding that of which one is accused
- Faith – believing obedience; taking a promise at face value, trusting in the pledge of a person that results in responsive action
- Flesh – the unregenerate state of men; the weaker element in human nature
- Glorification – to be magnified, extolled and praised
- Glory – to ascribe honor to; to praise
- Godliness – having a heart for God that manifests itself by living in such a way that is well-pleasing to the Lord
- Gospel – the good news
- Grace – God's unmerited favor and gifts to humanity
- Holiness – set apart and dedicated to God; pure, devoted
- Justification – to be declared or pronounced righteous; acquittal
- Law – God's commandments to Israel; Mosaic Law
- Peace – wholeness and well-being in all relationships
- Propitiation – the merciful means whereby God covers and passes over man's sin, atonement
- Redemption – to purchase with a view toward one's freedom; to release on receipt of ransom
- Repentance – a change of mind about something that one has been doing wrongly, coupled with a resolve to begin doing the right thing
- Righteousness – the state of being in the right, or declared to be"not guilty"
- Saints – all those who have been set apart, holy, dedicated to God

- Salvation – spiritual and eternal deliverance given immediately by God to those who accept His conditions of repentance and faith in Jesus Christ His Son
- Sanctification – separated to God; resulting in a believer's separation from evil things and evil ways, and his being empowered to realize the will of God in his life
- Sin – "missing the mark," disobedience to Divine law
- Soul – the breath of life; the immaterial, invisible part of man; the natural life of the body including perception, feelings, intellect, personality and desires
- Sovereign – above and superior to all; supreme in power, rank, and authority; holding the position of ruler; royalty
- Spirit – the life principle bestowed on man by God; an element similar to, but higher than the soul, affecting both the soul and the body
- Wrath – God's righteous response to evil, His refusal to condone unrighteousness and His judgment upon it

About the Author

Judy Gerry met the Lord Jesus Christ as her Savior when she was a young child. During her college years at the University of California at Riverside, Judy received training through the ministry of Campus Crusade for Christ. She attended their Institute of Biblical Studies where she received in-depth Bible training from some of the nation's top seminary professors. Those classes piqued her hunger for the Word of God.

In 1969 she graduated and joined the staff of Campus Crusade for Christ. She married Dave Gerry in 1971. By 1979, their lives were bustling as the parents of five youngsters. Realizing that children are a blessing from God, Dave and Judy relished the opportunity to love and train their children. Judy's greatest desire has always been to please the Lord by being a godly wife and mother. Today, all of their grown children are believers, and Judy and Dave agree that, "I have no greater joy than this, to hear of my children walking in the truth" (III John 4).

Judy and Dave were active on the board of directors for Child Evangelism Fellowship in Denver, Colorado, in the 1980s, and they were enthusiastic AWANA directors for many years. Judy continues to be active in her local "Moms-in-Touch" prayer group and mentoring "Mothers of Preschoolers."

She has been teaching and writing Bible studies for over thirty years. Her great delight is seeing believers experience the blessings of intimacy with the Lord, and victory in their lives, as they obediently follow God's "ancient paths" (Jeremiah 6:16).

Judy and Dave are enjoying their empty-nest years in Camarillo, California, as they mentor young families in their church, teach Bible studies, speak at retreats, delight in their grandchildren, and daily anticipate the return of the Lord Jesus Christ.

Acknowledgments

This book has been a team effort before a word of it was ever written. It was written in my heart by all who have mentored me in life through taking time to lovingly teach me; even when I didn't recognize my own ignorance.

I thank and praise the Lord for all of the "Barnabas" encouragers whom He has brought into my life.

Thank You, Lord, for parents and grandparents who provided both Dave and me with foundational instruction in godly living when we were youngsters.

Thank You, Lord, for our own children whose lives continue to exhort me in pursuing godliness.

Thank You, Lord, for my husband Dave's enthusiastic support, insightful ideas, and selfless patience when I was "in the zone" while writing.

Thank You, Lord, for the staff at the Camarillo Evangelical Free Church who gave me the freedom and encouragement to write and teach this Bible study.

Thank You, Lord, for the hundreds of women whose lives have been transformed through walking the Ancient Paths. Their lives have urged me on, and they have lovingly helped me with their suggestions and passion for biblical accuracy. These women have helped to prepare this study for publication.

Thank You, Lord, for servants like Pat Papenhausen whose tireless efforts to edit this series have yielded much fruit. For Elaine Lucas and Linda Campbell, who have been true cheerleaders in initiating and facilitating the teaching of *Ancient Paths for Modern Women*. For Leigh Anne Tsuji's expertise and commitment to enhancing the fruitfulness of this ministry. For Laurie Donahue, whose vision and impetus is making these materials widely available to women.

Thank You, Lord, for Your gifted servants, Dr. Howard Hendricks and for Nancy Leigh DeMoss, who selflessly encouraged me more than they will ever know.

Lord, thank You. May these study materials help the women of our generation find "rest for their souls" as they return to the Ancient Paths. This study is from You ... use it for Your purposes and pleasure.

"For from Him and through Him and to Him are all things.
To Him be the glory forever. Amen."
Romans 11:36

Ancient Paths Ministries

Ancient Paths Ministries is committed to redirecting contemporary culture back to the timeless truths of God's Word.

With an emphasis on the practical application of Scripture to everyday living, Dave and Judy Gerry provide Bible studies and resources for spiritual growth and maturity. As authors, Bible teachers, and conference speakers, they exhort others to pursue Jesus Christ and to know Him. It is through nurturing that relationship that one will discover the foundation of all issues of life.

In addition to speaking at men's and women's conferences, Dave and Judy also lead challenging weekend marriage retreats on "How to Have an Intentional Marriage."

For more information contact:

Dave and Judy Gerry
P.O. Box 498
Somis, CA 93066-0498
(805) 484-2808

E-mail: Judy@AncientPathsMinisitries.com
www.AncientPathsMinistries.com